Snake Lovers'
Lifelist and Journal

SNAKE LOVERS' LIFELIST & JOURNAL

by
Chris Scott

AUSTIN
UNIVERSITY OF TEXAS PRESS

Copyright © 1996
by the University
of Texas Press
All rights reserved

Printed in Hong Kong

First edition, 1996

Requests for permission
to reproduce material
from this work
should be sent to Permissions,
University of Texas Press,
Box 7819,
Austin, TX 78713-7819.

Cover photograph by Chris Scott

LIBRARY OF CONGRESS CATALOGING-IN-PUBLICATION DATA

Scott, Chris, 1961–
    Snake lovers' lifelist and journal / by Chris Scott. — 1st ed.
        p.   cm.
    Includes bibliographical references and index.
    ISBN 0-292-77698-5
    1. Snakes—United States.   2. Endangered species—United States.
I. Title.
QL666.O6S3915   1996
597.96'0973—dc20   95-32459

*This book
is dedicated
to the memory
of Pepere.*

CONTENTS

ACKNOWLEDGMENTS

THANKS go out to the following: Karen, for the great idea; my father, who first sparked my interest in these fascinating creatures and opened the door to understanding and appreciation rather than fear and destruction; my mother, who throughout my childhood years dealt with a plethora of creatures brought home in pillow cases, often to escape in her house; my grandmother and late grandfather, who often provided transportation to great snake-hunting locales and the very best companionship along the way; my son Matthew, who allows me to pass on to him the continued interest and concern for these misunderstood animals; and especially Lynn, who has accompanied me on many trips through swamps, deserts, and rugged mountains in some of the most remote areas of this country.

I want to thank R. D. "Dick" Bartlett, Walt Richardson, and Dan Fischer, who provided many of the "better" photographs used in this book. Each is an expert in his field as well as an outstanding nature photographer.

Finally, I thank Twila for her assistance in assembling the finished product and for providing proof that former snake "haters" can become snake "lovers."

Snake Lovers'
Lifelist and Journal

INTRODUCTION

MY CONCERN for the conservation of our native wildlife, particularly reptiles, began at a fairly early age; however, I came to this realization only after collaborating at the age of thirteen in an act that I have regretted ever since. When I was a child growing up in the suburbs of Baltimore, I met a man named Tom who worked at a local pet shop. At first I was impressed with this man, who was much older than I (in his thirties), because he had a remarkable knowledge of local reptiles and because he took the time to talk with me at length about these animals. Tom was especially interested in turtles and kept a large collection of native and exotic species at his house.

One day the conversation between Tom and me turned to the subject of Bog Turtles (*Clemmys muhlenbergii*), or Muhlenberg's Turtles, as they were called at that time. Tom told me that if I were ever to run across one, he would pay me fifty dollars for such a turtle. A year or two had passed when I discovered an adult Muhlenberg's Turtle in a small, spring-fed stream in northeastern Maryland. I'm not sure whether this species was protected by law at that time, but I suspected the reason Tom was willing to part with fifty dollars for this turtle must have been its rarity. Without taking time to think over the consequences, I contacted Tom and a meeting was arranged. After examining the beautiful turtle, Tom gladly paid me, with the agreement that I would show him where I had found it. Again, before considering the significance of his request, my greed and immaturity took over, and on the following day I took Tom to the "Muhlenberg" spring.

I have never seen or spoken to Tom since that day some twenty years ago, and I don't know if he cleaned out the spring run of this diminishing species, but it has been on my conscience ever since. The Bog Turtle is rapidly disappearing from much of its historical range, is considered endangered or threatened, and is protected in most states where it is found.

Through the years, I have seen the actions of humans (whether intentional or not) deplete populations of our native wildlife. I grew up listening to stories told by my father of the amazing diversity and abundance of wildlife in Florida. In 1981, I moved to Florida, where I became a park ranger stationed at various locations throughout the state. Over the years I witnessed firsthand the declining populations of native birds, reptiles, and mammals. Now, no more than fifty Florida Panthers are left in the wild, and

virtually all of Florida's gentle, slow-moving West Indian Mana-
tees are scarred by boat propellers. Florida has more species of endangered plants and animals than any other state. I remember a
sad day in the 1980s when the very last Dusky Seaside Sparrow
(*Ammodramus maritimus nigrescens*) ceased to exist and became
another statistic on the extinction list.

With every passing year, it seems more difficult to find an Eastern Diamondback Rattlesnake or Eastern Indigo Snake of significant size alive in the wild. In fact, the largest indigo snake I have
ever found was a 7-foot 7-inch roadkill specimen on Route 24 on
the way to Cedar Key in Levy County, Florida. Because I was able
to see this enormous creature from approximately one-half mile
away as I approached, I suspect that the killing of this serpent may
have been deliberate.

Florida, of course, is not the only state with an increasing number of species in danger of extinction. Unfortunately, in nearly every one of our states the list of endangered plants and animals is
increasing, often at an alarming rate. Human encroachment, destruction of habitats by development, and disturbance of wild
areas by such activities as road building, residential and industrial
construction, damming of rivers, depletion of wetlands, and various forms of pollution are all serious threats to our wildlife, especially reptiles and birds.

After spending a considerable amount of time in the Chiricahua
Mountains of Arizona and other Madrean mountain ranges of the
Southwest, I became aware that unscrupulous collectors are often
the most serious threat to many species of reptiles and birds of
prey indigenous to these unique ecological niches. Some falconers
will scale the heights of cliffs and canopies of trees to remove
young peregrine falcons, prairie falcons, and goshawks to be used
in their sport. In increasing numbers, greedy reptile collectors
tromp through the higher elevations of the picturesque mountains
to poach one or more of the three species of small montane rattlesnakes that are unique to these mountains and protected by Arizona law. I have learned that certain Europeans come to the southwestern United States with the intention of smuggling these
small rattlesnakes back to Europe where they can receive top dol-
lar for them. (Rattlesnakes are found only in the New World and
are much sought after by some foreign collectors.)

I have also learned that it is common knowledge among troops
stationed at several military bases in southern Arizona that they
can receive several hundred dollars each for ridgenose, banded
rock, and twin-spotted rattlesnakes. Undoubtedly, most of the
men and women serving in our armed forces respect and obey
laws pertaining to wildlife conservation, but a small minority of
unscrupulous collectors could eliminate these species from an
entire mountain range over a period of time.

"Extinction is forever" may be a cliché, but this is, after all, the
bottom line. To quote a recent publication from the U.S. Fish and
Wildlife Service: "Since the Pilgrims landed at Plymouth Rock,

more than 500 species and subspecies of our nation's plants and animals have become extinct, lost forever. By contrast, during the 3,000 years of the Pleistocene Ice Age, all of North America lost only 3 species every 100 years. The situation today is even worse in other parts of the world." If you become aware that someone is removing, selling, and/or killing a protected species, you should report that person to the Game and Fish Commission or the Department of Natural Resources in the state involved, or to the U.S. Fish and Wildlife Service.

It is difficult to believe that in this day and age several states, including Texas and Oklahoma, continue to permit legal "rattlesnake roundups" that are responsible for the deaths of tens of thousands, if not hundreds of thousands, of these animals every year. Neither snakes nor any other living creatures should be subjected to such cruelty. Snakes, especially venomous species, have been without a doubt among the most feared and persecuted of our native animals. Although I believe that respect and appreciation for many wild animals is slowly increasing along with a better understanding of the sensitivity of our ecosystems, it is also true that we have a long road ahead of us in our struggle for the environment.

It is my hope that Americans can learn to appreciate the value of our wilderness and its inhabitants before it's too late. Not long ago many state and county governments paid a bounty for every mountain lion killed. It is refreshing to know that now, the sight of a mountain lion in the wild is for many of us an awe inspiring sight that will forever be imprinted in our minds.

Those of us who are genuinely interested in reptiles and amphibians and are concerned about their welfare need to begin to adjust our thinking about how we practice our hobby of finding and studying these interesting creatures. I am of the belief that we should consider our avocation in a new light and should view this pastime as birders view theirs. A lifelist can be kept to record the species, subspecies, and various forms and phases observed in the wild. Rather than collecting specimens, we can locate, observe, appreciate, photograph, and/or document observations, and then move on, leaving the animal to live out its life in the wild. This transition from the old school of snake hunting, which often involved the taking of virtually every live serpent found, to be sold or kept captive until its death, to the more ecological practice of finding, photographing, and releasing is a welcome and needed change.

As a new herper, you will probably begin your lifelist with some of the more common and prolific species of your area. Soon you will find some of the less abundant and more secretive species. Before long you may, like a birder, find yourself traveling long distances to add one or two more species to your lifelist. It can become a very exciting and satisfying pastime. In portions of Florida, Texas, Arizona, and California, as many as thirty-plus species and subspecies of snakes may be found within a particular area; however, it can take years to find all of them. No matter where you call home, it will be a challenging task to locate in the wild every species of snake indigenous to your region.

When searching for snakes, care must be taken to disturb the environment as little as possible. Evidence of large-scale habitat destruction caused by unethical herptile collectors has been found in many states. It has been discovered that in Arizona and California commercial collectors have used such equipment as large crowbars, jackhammers and even dynamite to obtain Rosy Boas, Chuckwallas, and other cryptic species from their crevice domiciles. Sites where large-scale habitat destruction has been found include Organ Pipe Cactus National Monument in Arizona, where the collection of all wildlife is prohibited. Many times I have come across locations where it was obvious that others had been there weeks or even months before in search of snakes. Piles of wood had been moved and spread about, pieces of tin flipped in every direction, every bit of bark stripped from fallen trees, stumps torn apart. Sadly, I have witnessed, on more than one occasion, historical structures, including the famed "Hamburg Mine" structures, dismantled, apparently by individuals seeking montane rattlesnakes. Boards, rocks, tin, etc., often provide shelter and protection to living creatures including rodents, rabbits, amphibians, and a variety of insects. All cover, including natural and human-made shelter, must be returned to its original location after an exploration has been made.

Many reptile enthusiasts enjoy keeping one or more snakes in captivity. If you wish to keep snakes as pets, obtain the animals from captive breeding programs. Captive-bred snakes usually respond better to life in a cage and feed better than wild-caught snakes. These days, more and more species are available from captive breeding programs, including many subspecies and phases formerly considered rare. This is especially true with kingsnakes and ratsnakes. Some forms are far from inexpensive when obtained from an established captive breeding program; however acquiring them in this way will bring you the peace of mind that comes from knowing you have not strained the native population of that species.

A word of caution concerning the purchase of "captive bred" reptiles. While most reptile breeders are undoubtedly honest, reputable people with a genuine concern for our cold-blooded friends, some breeders/dealers have been known to sell animals they represent to be captive bred that are actually "wild caught." This is especially true with certain threatened, endangered, or otherwise protected species. Deceptive dealers have been known to sell over the course of a year thirty to forty Gila monsters that they claim on paper all came from a single pair of "legal" Gila monsters they possess. Female Gilas lay no more than eight eggs yearly. Please ask questions of the breeder to verify that the animal you intend to purchase is indeed captive bred. If the breeder is legitimate, as most are, he or she will not be offended.

Captive breeding is a tremendous boon to the hobby of herpeto-culture and no doubt benefits the environment by providing an alternative to field collecting wild animals. But, as with most good things, there is a down side. Unscrupulous collectors and poachers often use the "captive-bred" defense when explaining to the conservation officer why they have ten Rosy Boas in their possession while the legal bag limit for this species is two. In California, where the legal limit for Rosy Boas is two, the law sets no limits on the possession of "rosies" that are propagated in captivity. As you can imagine, it is often difficult or impossible to make a criminal case against someone who chooses to capitalize on this loophole to make a profit. We must hope that laws and the application of the laws protecting and preserving our native wildlife will become more stringent with fewer flaws while there are still some species left to protect! For information concerning captive breeding programs, you can contact your local herpetological association. You should, of course, look into state and local laws and ordinances pertaining to keeping captive snakes before obtaining any specimens.

USING THIS BOOK

THIS BOOK contains a comprehensive listing of 433 snake species, subspecies, intergrades, hybrids, and color phases found in the United States and Canada. Both native and introduced species have been included. The format of this lifelist is, with a few exceptions, in taxonomic order, which is the order utilized in most current field guides. Recording your observations of different species or forms on this lifelist will enable you to retain memories of a lifetime of herpetological field trips. Documenting the habitats, habits, size, sex, etc., of new forms will help you learn more about snakes in general.

COMMON NAMES: "Common" names of species, subspecies, and forms vary considerably from one geographical region to another. Many species have several common names, and several species may have the same common name. For example, in the northeastern United States, the term *blacksnake* is used when referring both to the Black Racer (*Coluber constrictor constrictor*) and the Black Rat Snake (*Elaphe obsoleta obsoleta*). Although these species are not closely related, they bear a superficial resemblance to one another and are therefore often called by the same name. For the same reason, species of the genus *Leptotyphlops*, or blind snakes, are often called worm snakes, as are species of the genus *Carphophis* (an eastern woodland snake).

Common names for various serpent species have changed with the times. I became interested in herpetology some twenty years ago after inheriting several snake books from my father, who is himself an amateur herpetologist. At that time I heard many species names that have since changed. Some examples are the Brown Snake, then called the DeKay's Snake; the Black Rat Snake, formerly known as the Pilot Black Snake; and the Coral Snake, previously identified as the Harlequin Snake.

For the purpose of this checklist, the common name is either the name used by a current field guide utilized for positive identification of the species or the name currently used by natives of the area where the species was found.

Among the several published lists of the correct common names for snake species, I prefer *Standard Common and Current Scientific Names for North American Amphibians and Reptiles,*

Third Edition, by Joseph T. Collins, editor and herpetologist, University of Kansas. Occasionally, however, the observer may encounter a color phase or newly discovered subspecies without a definitive common name. Common names often have more than one spelling—for example, Mohave and Mojave Rattlesnake. In recent years we have seen a trend toward shortening or simplifying common names. Examples are the hooknose snake, formerly *hook-nosed,* and the blackhead snake, formerly *black-headed.* I personally agree with simplifying the names.

In this book I have included several problematical forms that are not accepted by all herpetologists as subspecies, as well as several forms that were once recognized as subspecies but are no longer. An example of the latter would be the Coastal Plain Milk Snake (*Lampropeltis triangulum temporalis* or *Lampropeltis triangulum virginia*), formerly regarded as a distinct subspecies. It is now categorized as an intergrade between the Eastern Milk Snake (*Lampropeltis triangulum triangulum*) and the Scarlet Kingsnake (*Lampropeltis triangulum elapsoides*). It is interesting to note that whereas these two species coexist in a large area of northern Georgia, northern Alabama, Tennessee, Kentucky, and western North Carolina without the occurrence of this unusual color form, in the coastal plain region of New Jersey, Maryland, and Virginia this form is the indigenous milk snake of the area. To my knowledge, no pure Eastern Milk Snake or Scarlet Kingsnake has been found in this area. Having found one of these jewels in the wild, I am of the opinion that it should be recognized as a distinct form (at least for the purpose of a lifelist). Although the Coastal Plain Milk Snake most closely resembles the Scarlet Kingsnake in appearance, size, and habits, it is quite different from the "field guide" description of either form. For the same reason a birder would include both the yellow-shafted and red-shafted race of the flicker on his lifelist, I have included the Coastal Plain Milk Snake as well as the light and dark phases of the Timber Rattlesnake, etc.

SCIENTIFIC NAMES: Scientific or Latin names for snakes can be at least as controversial as common names. The scientific name is used to make a positive identification and documentation of a species. Many scientific names or parts of scientific names (particularly genera) have changed in recent years. Some examples are the water snakes, formerly genus *Natrix* and now broken up into the genera *Nerodia, Regina,* and *Clonophis.* Snakes of the genus *Elaphe* are now divided into *Elaphe, Bogertophis,* and *Senticolis.* Despite the changes, it is fairly easy to trace these names through textbooks to identify species, subspecies, and forms. Some very distinct forms of such species as the Blotched Kingsnake or the Coastal Plain Milk Snake no longer enjoy their own subspecies designations but are simply considered forms of a particular subspecies.

Scientific names consist of two or three parts: genus, species, and sometimes subspecies. A complete classification would include the following:

(1) Class	(4) Suborder	(7) Genus
(2) Subclass	(5) Family	(8) Species
(3) Order	(6) Subfamily	(9) Subspecies

For the purpose of this journal, only the last five will be used. All snakes fall into the class Reptilia, order Squamata and suborder Serpentes.

The genus is the first word in the scientific name. A genus consists of a number of closely related species, all of which share the same generic name.

Members of a species, which often comprises numerous subspecies, are generally very much alike and can interbreed; however they rarely interbreed with another species to produce fertile offspring. Where a certain species occurs over a wide range, animals at one end of the range may differ in appearance, size, etc., from those at the other. Over time, changes in the environment or other factors may result in isolated populations of a species in areas such as "sky islands," which are desert mountains separated by distances from the remainder of the population. These changes may result in the eventual evolution of a new species or subspecies.

The word *subspecies* indicates a unique race or form of a species. If a scientific name has only two parts (a binomial), such as *Crotalus adamanteus* (Eastern Diamondback Rattlesnake), then no subspecies of this species are known. When a scientific name has three parts (a trinomial), that tells us that two or more subspecies have been named. An example is the Arizona Black Rattlesnake (*Crotalus viridis cerberus*), which is a subspecies of the Western Rattlesnake (*Crotalus viridis viridis*):

(1) *Crotalus* indicates a GENUS of rattlesnake.
(2) *viridis* indicates a SPECIES of Western Rattlesnake.
(3) *cerberus* indicates the SUBSPECIES Arizona Black Rattlesnake.

As with common names, many species or subspecies designations honor particular persons, usually herpetologists or other naturalists. The Banded Rock Rattlesnake, *Crotalus lepidus klauberi*, for example, was probably identified by L. M. Klauber, a herpetologist of the early to mid-twentieth century, and *Elaphe bairdi*, the Baird's Rat Snake, was named after S. F. Baird, who catalogued the Smithsonian's reptile collection in 1853. This should inspire many up-and-coming herpetologists.

DATE: The date and time when a species was observed.

LOCATION: Careful and precise notes should be taken as to the exact location where a species is caught or seen. These notes will help to establish range extensions and/or distributions of species. Unfortunately, more and more species are becoming rare due to habitat destruction, human encroachment in wild areas, overcollection, pollution, etc.

Careful record keeping and note taking may help with future efforts to preserve and protect species in the wild.

HABITAT: The habitat is the particular type of environment in which the species lives, such as a salt marsh or a rocky hillside. Some species of snakes are habitat specialists; the Banded Sand Snake (*Chilomeniscus cinctus*), for example, requires a desert habitat with fine sand to "swim" in. Other species are habitat generalists, such as the Eastern Garter Snake (*Thamnophis sirtalis sirtalis*), which is found in a variety of habitats ranging from streamsides to dry woodlands, city lots, and mountainsides.

Because many serpent species are habitat specialists and therefore restricted to a specific limited environment, knowing precisely where a specimen was found can be useful when trying to identify it. For instance, you find a snake in the forested Arizona mountains at an altitude of 7,500 feet that is banded with black, red, and yellowish white. Although superficially it resembles the Arizona Coral Snake (Micruroides euryxanthus), you can rule out that species based on habitat and altitude. This snake would be an Arizona Mountain Kingsnake (Lampropeltis pyromelana). Conversely, recognizing types of habitats can assist in locating a particular snake species.

WEATHER: Include temperature, humidity, precipitation, amount of cloud cover, sunlight, moonlight, and wind activity. Many snake species indigenous to desert regions become active only after the summer monsoons have begun and can only be found in significant numbers a few nights of the year. It is also interesting to note that snakes are found crossing the roads at night in much smaller numbers when it is windy or when there is a full moon. Recording weather conditions makes it easier to establish times and weather conditions in which different species of snakes are most active.

Keeping records of temperatures and weather conditions when snakes are found will also show you that some snake species are much more cold- or heat-tolerant than others. While on a week-long trip to Arizona in May 1992, I was fortunate to locate and photograph seven species of rattlesnakes in seven days. We had enjoyed warm, sunny days until the day before my departure, when the weather suddenly turned cold and rainy. It was May 23 (which was also my birthday) and I was visiting the Chiricahua Mountains, a herpetologist's paradise. Around noon I was at 8,500 feet elevation, the temperature was at most 60 degrees Fahrenheit, it was raining, and I was dressed in three layers of clothing in a last-ditch effort to find and photograph a Twin-spotted Rattlesnake (*Crotalus pricei*). This species was the last needed to complete my wish list. I knew I was in the right habitat, so I had decided to try, although I thought that finding a Twin-spot (or any reptile) under those circumstances would be about like winning the lottery. I parked the rental car and walked no more than 300 feet up a talus slope. There I discovered a beautiful, two-foot-long Twin-spot coiled on top of a rock. Due to the very short season of warm weather at such high altitudes, these snakes have become more cold tolerant than other species. On the other end of the temperature-adjustment continuum, diurnal coachwhip and whipsnakes (*Masticophis*) and patchnose (*Salvadora*) snakes are able to remain active in the deserts when the temperature approaches 100 degrees Fahrenheit.

REMARKS: In this section you can describe specimens with unusual coloration or markings. Many strange color forms or unusually marked specimens may not be illustrated in some field guides or even mentioned in others. Trying to identify one of these irregular snakes in the field can be very confusing.

While road hunting one August night in the Catalina Foothills near Sabino Canyon in Tucson, I discovered two unusually colored snakes that after careful examination were identified as Western Longnose Snakes (*Rhinocheilus lecontei lecontei*). The first was D.O.R. (dead on road) and was approximately 9 inches long. When I first saw this snake in my headlights, I thought it was a Saddled Leafnose Snake (*Phyllorhynchus browni browni*). Just over the next hill, I discovered a live snake crossing the road that was identical to the D.O.R. but less than 20 inches long. Both snakes were cream colored with brownish black blotches but no red coloration at all. I later learned that this localized color form, once regarded as a distinct subspecies (*Rhinocheilus lecontei clarus*), is common in the foothills north of Tucson, as well as other areas of the Sonoran Desert. Some other unusual color forms I have discovered are the bright orange Northern Banded Water Snake (*Nerodia sipedon*) and Eastern Garter Snake (*Thamnophis sirtalis sirtalis*) with no stripes.

Several species, including the Gray-banded Kingsnake (*Lampropeltis alterna*), California Kingsnake (*Lampropeltis getulus californiae*), and Ground Snake *(Sonora semiannulata)*, are highly variable in color and pattern. When unusual-looking specimens are found, their appearance should be well documented and they should be photographed if possible.

It is also useful to note unusual or rarely witnessed behaviors in wild snakes, such as mating, death feigning, tail shaking, etc. Notes should also be taken concerning temperament. Many factors can alter the way a snake behaves, including temperature, time of day or season, or whether the snake is in shed, has just eaten, or has been injured. Many a snake hunter has suffered the unfortunate experience of handling a snake that has just eaten and having that meal regurgitated on him. Some snakes, such as the genus *Nerodia*, water snakes, are known for their pugnacious and nasty dispositions while other species, including the Hognose Snake (*Heterodon* sp.), can usually be relied upon to be mild mannered and passive.

STATUS: In the case of species, subspecies, and forms that are protected by state or federal law, and many are, the protected status and the area where they are protected are listed with the notation **DO NOT COLLECT: PROTECTED SPECIES**. The terms used to describe the status vary from state to state and include the following:

Endangered
Threatened
Protected
Species of special concern
Extirpated
Watchlist species
Candidate species
Rare, Rare and declining, or Rare and local
Sensitive
Imperiled

The definitions of regulatory terms may vary as much in different states as do the terms themselves. Generally, the terms *endangered, threatened,* and *protected* indicate that the animal is fully protected. The term *extirpated* means that the species is believed to be extinct within that state; however, this term usually goes hand-in-hand with the word *endangered,* indicating that any populations that may still be found are protected. The term *species of special concern* in some states means that the species is protected, while in other states this designation does not protect the animal. *Candidate* species are not usually protected; however, they are under consideration for a protected status. *Watchlist* species are much like candidate species. Animals listed as *rare, rare and declining, rare and local,* or *imperiled* may or may not be protected, depending on the state. The term *sensitive* is used by several states; this listing generally does not afford the species protection, but usually indicates that the species is vulnerable to over collection, habitat destruction, etc. Federally protected species are protected throughout the United States. Laws protecting wildlife, both state and federal, often prohibit disturbing or harassing protected species, which may even extend to photographing an animal. Many states require a fishing or hunting license, or some other permit, to collect nonprotected species; and bag limits come into play. Some states also prohibit the sale, purchase, trade, etc., of native species.

You should be aware that if while on vacation in a neighboring state you collect a reptile in violation of any law, whether it be local, state or federal, and you transport this animal back to your home state, you are in violation of the federal Lacey Act. It is your responsibility to familiarize yourself with regulatory laws pertaining to reptiles in each area you visit. Yes, these laws can be confusing, but they are good laws, enacted to preserve our native species. When in doubt, DO NOT COLLECT!

INTERGRADES AND HYBRIDS

HYBRIDS ARE produced when individuals of two different species mate successfully. An example of a hybrid is the offspring of a Banded Rock Rattlesnake (*Crotalus lepidus klauberi*) and an Animas Ridgenose Rattlesnake (*Crotalus willardi obscurus*). Intergrades occur when two different subspecies of the same species breed and produce offspring. An example of an intergrade would be the offspring of an Eastern Cottonmouth (*Agkistrodon piscivorus piscivorus*) and a Western Cottonmouth (*Agkistrodon piscivorus leucostoma*). Intergrades occur more commonly than hybrids. This section is a list of selected intergrades and hybrids that I felt would be of particular interest to readers. Many intergrades and hybrids are known to occur in areas of overlapping ranges between closely related species and subspecies that are very similar in appearance, habits, and habitats. Because of this I have not included the majority of intergrades and hybrids in the main part of the text. All of the hybrids and intergrade forms described have been recorded from reliable sources as occurring naturally in the wild.

California Rosy Boa / Arizona Rosy Boa (INTERGRADE)
Lichanura trivirgata myriolepis / Lichanura trivirgata arizonia

DATE, LOCATION, REMARKS:

California Rosy Boa / Coastal Rosy Boa (INTERGRADE)
Lichanura trivirgata myriolepis / Lichanura trivirgata roseofusca

DATE, LOCATION, REMARKS:

Northern Water Snake / Midland Water Snake (INTERGRADE)
Nerodia sipedon sipedon / Nerodia sipedon pleuralis

DATE, LOCATION, REMARKS:

Northern Water Snake / Banded Water Snake (HYBRID)
Nerodia sipedon sipedon / Nerodia fasciata fasciata

DATE, LOCATION, REMARKS:

Banded Water Snake / Midland Water Snake (HYBRID)
Nerodia fasciata fasciata / Nerodia sipedon pleuralis

DATE, LOCATION, REMARKS:

Banded Water Snake / Carolina Salt Marsh Snake (HYBRID)
Nerodia fasciata fasciata / Nerodia sipedon williamengelsi

DATE, LOCATION, REMARKS:

Banded Water Snake / Broad-banded Water Snake (INTERGRADE)
Nerodia fasciata fasciata / Nerodia fasciata confluens

DATE, LOCATION, REMARKS:

Gulf Salt Marsh Snake / Banded Water Snake (HYBRID)
Nerodia clarkii clarkii / Nerodia fasciata fasciata

DATE, LOCATION, REMARKS:

Mangrove Salt Marsh Snake / Florida Banded Water Snake (HYBRID)
Nerodia clarkii compressicauda / Nerodia fasciata pictiventris

DATE, LOCATION, REMARKS:

Northern Redbelly Snake / Black Hills Redbelly Snake (INTERGRADE)
Storeria occipitomaculata occipitomaculata / Storeria occipitomaculata pahasapae

DATE, LOCATION, REMARKS:

Western Ribbon Snake / Arid Land Ribbon Snake (INTERGRADE)
Thamnophis proximus proximus / Thamnophis proximus diabolicus

DATE, LOCATION, REMARKS:

Western Ribbon Snake / Redstripe Ribbon Snake (INTERGRADE)
Thamnophis proximus proximus / Thamnophis proximus rubrilineatus

DATE, LOCATION, REMARKS:

Redstripe Ribbon Snake / Arid Land Ribbon Snake (INTERGRADE)
Thamnophis proximus rubrilineatus / Thamnophis proximus diabolicus

DATE, LOCATION, REMARKS:

Gulf Coast Ribbon Snake / Western Ribbon Snake (INTERGRADE)
Thamnophis proximus orarius / Thamnophis proximus proximus

DATE, LOCATION, REMARKS:

Gulf Coast Ribbon Snake / Arid Land Ribbon Snake (INTERGRADE)
Thamnophis proximus orarius / Thamnophis proximus diabolicus

DATE, LOCATION, REMARKS:

Gulf Coast Ribbon Snake / Redstripe Ribbon Snake (INTERGRADE)
Thamnophis proximus orarius / Thamnophis proximus rubrilineatus

DATE, LOCATION, REMARKS:

Santa Cruz Garter Snake / Two-striped Garter Snake (HYBRID)
Thamnophis couchi atratus / Thamnophis hammondii

DATE, LOCATION, REMARKS:

Oregon Garter Snake / Sierra Garter Snake (INTERGRADE)
Thamnophis couchi hydrophilus / Thamnophis couchi couchi

DATE, LOCATION, REMARKS:

Dusty Hognose Snake / Plains Hognose Snake (INTERGRADE)
Heterodon nasicus gloydi / Heterodon nasicus nasicus

DATE, LOCATION, REMARKS:

Northern Ringneck Snake / Southern Ringneck Snake (INTERGRADE)
Diadophis punctatus edwardsi / Diadophis punctatus punctatus

This intergrade is commonly encountered in the Delmarva Peninsula and in southern New Jersey.

DATE, LOCATION, REMARKS:

Regal Ringneck Snake / Prairie Ringneck Snake (INTERGRADE)
Diadophis punctatus regalis / Diadophis punctatus arnyi

DATE, LOCATION, REMARKS:

Eastern Worm Snake / Midwest Worm Snake (INTERGRADE)
Carphophis amoenus amoenus / Carphophis amoenus helenae

DATE, LOCATION, REMARKS:

Western Worm Snake / Midwest Worm Snake (HYBRID)
Carphophis vermis / Carphophis amoenus helenae

This hybrid has been found in northeastern Louisiana.

DATE, LOCATION, REMARKS:

Eastern Mud Snake / Western Mud Snake (INTERGRADE)
Farancia abacura abacura / Farancia abacura reinwardti

DATE, LOCATION, REMARKS:

Eastern Yellowbelly Racer / Mexican Racer (INTERGRADE)
Coluber constrictor flaviventris / Coluber constrictor oaxaca

DATE, LOCATION, REMARKS:

Eastern Yellowbelly Racer / Western Yellowbelly Racer (INTERGRADE)
Coluber constrictor flaviventris / Coluber constrictor mormon

This intergrade has been found in central Wyoming.

DATE, LOCATION, REMARKS:

Western Coachwhip / Lined Coachwhip Snake (INTERGRADE)
Masticophis flagellum testaceus / Masticophis flagellum lineatulus

DATE, LOCATION, REMARKS:

Ruthven's Whipsnake / Schott's Whipsnake (INTERGRADE)
Masticophis taeniatus ruthveni / Masticophis taeniatus schotti

DATE, LOCATION, REMARKS:

Mountain Patchnose Snake / Texas Patchnose Snake (INTERGRADE)
Salvadora grahamiae grahamiae / Salvadora grahamiae lineata

This intergrade has been found in west central Texas.

DATE, LOCATION, REMARKS

Corn Snake / Great Plains Rat Snake (INTERGRADE)
Elaphe guttata guttata / Elaphe guttata emoryi

DATE, LOCATION, REMARKS:

Corn Snake / Yellow Rat Snake (HYBRID)
Elaphe guttata guttata / Elaphe obsoleta quadrivitta

DATE, LOCATION, REMARKS:

Northern Pine Snake / Florida Pine Snake (INTERGRADE)
Pituophis melanoleucus melanoleucus / Pituophis melanoleucus mugitus

DATE, LOCATION, REMARKS:

Desert Kingsnake / Speckled Kingsnake (INTERGRADE)
Lampropeltis getulus splendida / Lampropeltis getulus holbrooki

DATE, LOCATION, REMARKS:

Desert Kingsnake / California Kingsnake (INTERGRADE)
Lampropeltis getulus splendida / Lampropeltis getulus californiae

DATE, LOCATION, REMARKS:

Desert Kingsnake / Mexican Black Kingsnake (INTERGRADE)
Lampropeltis getulus splendida / Lampropeltis getulus nigritus

DATE, LOCATION, REMARKS:

Mole Kingsnake / Prairie Kingsnake (INTERGRADE)
Lampropeltis calligaster rhombomaculata / Lampropeltis calligaster calligaster

DATE, LOCATION, REMARKS:

Gray-banded Kingsnake / New Mexico Milksnake (HYBRID)
Lampropeltis alterna / Lampropeltis triangulum celaenops

DATE, LOCATION, REMARKS:

Northern Copperhead / Southern Copperhead (INTERGRADE)
Agkistrodon contortrix mokeson / Agkistrodon contortrix contortrix

DATE, LOCATION, REMARKS:

Northern Copperhead / Osage Copperhead (INTERGRADE)
Agkistrodon contortrix mokeson / Agkistrodon contortrix phaeogaster

DATE, LOCATION, REMARKS:

Osage Copperhead / Southern Copperhead (INTERGRADE)
Agkistrodon contortrix phaeogaster / Agkistrodon contortrix contortrix

DATE, LOCATION, REMARKS:

Southern Copperhead / Broad-banded Copperhead (INTERGRADE)
Agkistrodon contortrix contortrix / Agkistrodon contortrix laticinctus

DATE, LOCATION, REMARKS:

Northern Copperhead / Broad-banded Copperhead (INTERGRADE)
Agkistrodon contortrix mokeson / Agkistrodon contortrix laticinctus

DATE, LOCATION, REMARKS:

Broad-banded Copperhead / Osage Copperhead (INTERGRADE)
Agkistrodon contortrix laticinctus / Agkistrodon contortrix phaeogaster

DATE, LOCATION, REMARKS:

Trans-Pecos Copperhead / Broad-banded Copperhead (INTERGRADE)
Agkistrodon contortrix pictigaster / Agkistrodon contortrix laticinctus

DATE, LOCATION, REMARKS:

Eastern Cottonmouth / Florida Cottonmouth (INTERGRADE)
Agkistrodon piscivorus piscivorus / Agkistrodon piscivorus conanti

DATE, LOCATION, REMARKS:

Eastern Cottonmouth / Western Cottonmouth (INTERGRADE)
Agkistrodon piscivorus piscivorus / Agkistrodon piscivorus leucostoma

DATE, LOCATION, REMARKS:

Eastern Massasauga / Western Massasauga (INTERGRADE)
Sistrurus catenatus catenatus / Sistrurus catenatus tergeminus

DATE, LOCATION, REMARKS:

Western Massasauga / Desert Massasauga (INTERGRADE)
Sistrurus catenatus tergeminus / Sistrurus catenatus edwardsi

DATE, LOCATION, REMARKS:

Eastern Massasauga / Timber Rattlesnake (HYBRID)
Sistrurus catenatus catenatus / Crotalus horridus horridus

DATE, LOCATION, REMARKS:

Carolina Pigmy Rattlesnake / Dusky Pigmy Rattlesnake (INTERGRADE)
Sistrurus miliarius miliarius / Sistrurus miliarius barbouri

DATE, LOCATION, REMARKS:

Carolina Pigmy Rattlesnake / Western Pigmy Rattlesnake (INTERGRADE)
Sistrurus miliarius miliarius / Sistrurus miliarius streckeri

DATE, LOCATION, REMARKS:

Western Pigmy Rattlesnake / Dusky Pigmy Rattlesnake (INTERGRADE)
Sistrurus miliarius streckeri / Sistrurus miliarius barbouri

DATE, LOCATION, REMARKS:

Eastern Diamondback Rattlesnake / Canebrake (Timber) Rattlesnake (HYBRID)
Crotalus adamanteus / Crotalus horridus atricaudatus

DATE, LOCATION, REMARKS:

Red Diamond Rattlesnake / Southern Pacific Rattlesnake (HYBRID)

Crotalus ruber / Crotalus viridis helleri

DATE, LOCATION, REMARKS:

Mojave Rattlesnake / Southern Pacific Rattlesnake (HYBRID)

Crotalus scutulatus / Crotalus viridis helleri

A number of these hybrids have been reported from Antelope Valley, California.

DATE, LOCATION, REMARKS:

Mojave Rattlesnake / Prairie Rattlesnake (HYBRID)

Crotalus scutulatus / Crotalus viridis viridis

A number of these hybrids have been encountered in Hudspeth County, Texas, and in south central New Mexico.

DATE, LOCATION, REMARKS:

Western Diamondback Rattlesnake / Northern Blacktail Rattlesnake (HYBRID)

Crotalus atrox atrox / Crotalus molossus molossus

DATE, LOCATION, REMARKS:

Animas Ridgenose / Banded Rock Rattlesnake (HYBRID)
Crotalus willardi obscurus / Crotalus lepidus klauberi

This hybrid is found in the Sky Islands of southeastern Arizona and southwestern New Mexico.

DATE, LOCATION, REMARKS:

BLIND SNAKES

Families: Typhlopidae and Leptotyphlopidae
Genera: *Ramphotyphlops* and *Leptotyphlops*

THESE TWO families of very small subterranean burrowers contain approximately 250 species worldwide in four genera. They are the smallest of our snakes and may superficially resemble earthworms. The species *Ramphotyphlops braminus*, a unisexual member of the family Typhlopidae, is not native to the United States but has been introduced to several areas of southern Florida, Mexico, and Hawaii from Asia. The family Leptotyphlopidae, represented in the United States by the genus *Leptotyphlops*, are generally found in the south central and southwestern United States. In the United States, these species range in length from 4⅛ inches to approximately 16 inches and are very slender. These snakes are generally nocturnal and spend most of their lives below ground.

Brahminy Blind Snake
Ramphotyphlops braminus

This tiny Asian species has been introduced into southern Florida and Hawaii, as well as many other parts of the world, and is now established in some areas.

DATE:

LOCATION:

HABITAT:

WEATHER:

SIZE/SEX:

REMARKS:

DATE:

LOCATION:

HABITAT:

WEATHER:

SIZE/SEX:

REMARKS:

Western Blind Snake, Southwestern Blind Snake
Leptotyphlops humilis humilis

DATE:

LOCATION:

HABITAT:

WEATHER:

SIZE/SEX:

REMARKS:

Utah Blind Snake
Leptotyphlops humilis utahensis

STATUS: Candidate, endangered and threatened species listing, State of Utah

---

DATE:

LOCATION:

HABITAT:

WEATHER:

SIZE/SEX:

REMARKS:

Trans-Pecos Blind Snake
Leptotyphlops humilis segregus

Desert Blind Snake
Leptotyphlops humilis cahuilae

DATE:

LOCATION:

HABITAT:

WEATHER:

SIZE/SEX:

REMARKS:

Texas Blind Snake
Leptotyphlops dulcis dulcis

DATE:

LOCATION:

HABITAT:

WEATHER:

SIZE/SEX:

REMARKS:

New Mexico Blind Snake
Leptotyphlops dulcis dissectus

STATUS: THREATENED,
State of Kansas
**DO NOT COLLECT:
PROTECTED SPECIES**

DATE:

LOCATION:

HABITAT:

WEATHER:

SIZE/SEX:

REMARKS:

DATE:

LOCATION:

HABITAT:

WEATHER:

SIZE/SEX:

REMARKS:

**Additional species,
subspecies, and forms**

COMMON NAME:

SCIENTIFIC NAME:

DATE:

LOCATION:

HABITAT:

WEATHER:

SIZE/SEX:

REMARKS:

COMMON NAME:

SCIENTIFIC NAME:

DATE:

LOCATION:

HABITAT:

WEATHER:

SIZE/SEX:

REMARKS:

COMMON NAME:

SCIENTIFIC NAME:

BOAS AND PYTHONS

Family: *Boidae*
Genera: *Charina* and *Lichanura*

THIS FAMILY of mostly tropical snakes is represented in the United States by only two native genera, rubber boas (*Charina*) and rosy boas (*Lichanura*). This large family includes the well-known boa constrictors and pythons, which are among the world's largest snakes with species occasionally exceeding 30 feet in length. Both species found in the United States are much smaller, seldom exceeding 3 feet. Pythons are found mainly in the Old World and are oviparous. Boas are viviparous and are found in both the New World and the Old. Boas are among the most primitive of snakes; males often have vestiges of hind limbs (spurs) present just above the tail on each side of the vent. Some species have temperature sensitive pits on the labial scales which assist them in finding warm-blooded prey. All species have elliptical pupils.

An increasing number of boa constrictors and pythons of several species have been observed, captured, or killed in many areas of this country—particularly South Florida—that appear to be escaped captives. It is possible, but rather unlikely, that breeding populations have been established.

DATE: **Pacific Rubber Boa**
                                                    Charina bottae bottae
LOCATION:

HABITAT:

WEATHER:

SIZE/SEX:

REMARKS:

DATE: **Rocky Mountain
                                                    Rubber Boa**
LOCATION: *Charina bottae utahensis*

HABITAT:

WEATHER:

SIZE/SEX:

REMARKS:

DATE: **Southern California
                                                    Rubber Boa**
LOCATION: *Charina bottae umbratica*

HABITAT: STATUS: THREATENED,
                                                    State of California
WEATHER: CANDIDATE, Federal en-
                                                    dangered or threatened
SIZE/SEX: species listing
                                                    **DO NOT COLLECT:
REMARKS: PROTECTED SPECIES**

Coastal Rosy Boa
Lichanura trivirgata roseofusca

STATUS: CANDIDATE, Federal endangered or threatened species listing

In the United States, this form is found only in extreme southern California, and most specimens encountered north of the Mexican border are intergrades with *Lichanura trivirgata myriolepis.*

DATE:

LOCATION:

HABITAT:

WEATHER:

SIZE/SEX:

REMARKS:

California Rosy Boa (coastal phase)
Lichanura trivirgata myriolepis

This form, found in appropriate habitat in southern California, generally west of true desert habitats, has stripes that are usually poorly defined. Ground color is usually bluish gray.

DATE:

LOCATION:

HABITAT:

WEATHER:

SIZE/SEX:

REMARKS:

California Rosy Boa (desert phase)
Lichanura trivirgata myriolepis

Formerly recognized as *Lichanura trivirgata gracia,* this form has stripes with more distinct borders than the coastal phase. This morph is found in appropriate habitat in the desert regions of southern California and extreme southwestern Arizona.

DATE:

LOCATION:

HABITAT:

WEATHER:

SIZE/SEX:

REMARKS:

This newly described subspecies appears to be valid. Possibly the most attractive *trivirgata*, this subspecies usually has a tan ground color with well-defined brown stripes. It is restricted in range to several desert mountain ranges of northwestern Arizona.

Arizona Rosy Boa
Lichanura trivirgata arizonae

DATE:

LOCATION:

HABITAT:

WEATHER:

SIZE/SEX:

REMARKS:

It is interesting to note that although this subspecies is not protected as a species, its entire known range in the United States is on National Park Service or National Wildlife Refuge lands where reptile collecting is illegal. This subspecies is commonly sold at pet shops and expos throughout the country. Before purchasing or otherwise obtaining a Mexican Rosy Boa, inquire as to its origin.

Mexican Rosy Boa
Lichanura trivirgata trivirgata

DATE:

LOCATION:

HABITAT:

WEATHER:

SIZE/SEX:

REMARKS:

DATE:

LOCATION:

HABITAT:

WEATHER:

SIZE/SEX:

REMARKS:

Additional species, subspecies, and forms

COMMON NAME:

SCIENTIFIC NAME:

COLUBRIDS
Family: Colubridae

THIS LARGEST of all snake families includes almost 85 percent of the snakes found in the United States. Members of this family vary considerably in appearance, size, habits, etc. Colubrids may have round or elliptical pupils; scales may be smooth or keeled. Some colubrids are rear fanged and capable of injecting venom, but most are considered harmless to humans.

In the United States, this family includes semiaquatic to near truly aquatic forms such as garter snakes (*Thamnophis*), water snakes (*Nerodia*), and crayfish snakes (*Regina*); terrestrial forms including kingsnakes (*Lampropeltis*) and gopher snakes (*Pituophis*); and several somewhat arboreal species including rat snakes (*Elaphe*) and green snakes (*Opheodrys*). Colubrids vary in size from the tiny earth snakes (*Virginia*) and blackhead snakes (*Tantilla*), which are usually well under a foot in length as adults, to the indigo snakes (*Drymarchon*), which can exceed 8 feet. The majority of species are oviparous, while others are viviparous.

Worldwide, colubrids make up approximately three-fourths of snake species and are found on all continents except Antarctica.

WATER SNAKES AND SALT MARSH SNAKES

Family: Colubridae
Genus: *Nerodia* (formerly *Natrix*)

NERODIA ARE generally medium to large, thick-bodied, semi-aquatic snakes. The greatest number of species are found in the southeastern and south central United States, but *Nerodia* can occur as far west as Colorado, Texas, and Baja California in Mexico and as far north as Maine and southern Canada. This genus is restricted to the United States and Mexico, with one species found on the northern coast of Cuba. Many forms are confused with the venomous cottonmouths (*Agkistrodon*) and are often killed for this reason.

Most forms are heavy bodied with large heads and keeled scales. When found in the wild, many individuals are quick to bite, although some settle down soon after capture and permit handling. The reader should be aware that some *Nerodia* species are apt to discharge a foul-smelling musk from the anal vent after capture.

Although some people believe that water snakes compete with fishermen for game fish in our rivers and lakes, they actually improve fishing by feeding on less vigorous and diseased fish. By keeping those bodies of water from being overpopulated with stunted fish, water snakes allow healthy fish to become trophy fish.

Mississippi Green Water Snake

Nerodia cyclopion

STATUS: ENDANGERED, State of Kentucky
THREATENED, State of Illinois
EXTIRPATED, State of Missouri
DO NOT COLLECT: PROTECTED SPECIES

DATE:

LOCATION:

HABITAT:

WEATHER:

SIZE/SEX:

REMARKS:

Florida Green Water Snake

Nerodia floridana

Color may be somewhat variable throughout range.

DATE:

LOCATION:

HABITAT:

WEATHER:

SIZE/SEX:

REMARKS:

Florida Green Water Snake (reddish phase)

Nerodia floridana

Reddish individuals are encountered fairly often in southern Florida.

DATE:

LOCATION:

HABITAT:

WEATHER:

SIZE/SEX:

REMARKS:

DATE:

LOCATION:

HABITAT:

WEATHER:

SIZE/SEX:

REMARKS:

Brown Water Snake
Nerodia taxispilota

DATE:

LOCATION:

HABITAT:

WEATHER:

SIZE/SEX:

REMARKS:

**Diamondback
Water Snake**
*Nerodia rhombifer
rhombifer*

STATUS: THREATENED,
State of Iowa
**DO NOT COLLECT:
PROTECTED SPECIES**

DATE:

LOCATION:

HABITAT:

WEATHER:

SIZE/SEX:

REMARKS:

Redbelly Water Snake
*Nerodia erythrogaster
erythrogaster*

Copperbelly Water Snake

Nerodia erythrogaster neglecta

STATUS: ENDANGERED, states of Ohio and Michigan; THREATENED, State of Indiana; SPECIES OF SPECIAL CONCERN, State of Kentucky; CANDIDATE, Federal endangered or threatened species listing
DO NOT COLLECT: PROTECTED SPECIES

DATE:

LOCATION:

HABITAT:

WEATHER:

SIZE/SEX:

REMARKS:

Yellowbelly Water Snake

Nerodia erythrogaster flavigaster

STATUS: ENDANGERED, State of Iowa
DO NOT COLLECT: PROTECTED SPECIES

DATE:

LOCATION:

HABITAT:

WEATHER:

SIZE/SEX:

REMARKS:

Blotched Water Snake

Nerodia erythrogaster transversa

STATUS: ENDANGERED, State of New Mexico, Group 2
DO NOT COLLECT: PROTECTED SPECIES

Pattern and/or color may be extremely variable throughout range.

DATE:

LOCATION:

HABITAT:

WEATHER:

SIZE/SEX:

REMARKS:

Pattern and/or color may be extremely variable throughout range.

DATE:

LOCATION:

HABITAT:

WEATHER:

SIZE/SEX:

REMARKS:

Northern Water Snake, Northern Banded Water Snake
Nerodia sipedon sipedon

DATE:

LOCATION:

HABITAT:

WEATHER:

SIZE/SEX:

REMARKS:

Lake Erie Water Snake
Nerodia sipedon insularum

STATUS: CANDIDATE, Federal endangered or threatened species listing

---

This very dark subspecies is restricted in distribution to the Outer Banks of North Carolina where it is found in salt and brackish water habitats.

DATE:

LOCATION:

HABITAT:

WEATHER:

SIZE/SEX:

REMARKS:

Carolina Salt Marsh Snake
Nerodia sipedon williamengelsi

STATUS: SPECIES OF SPECIAL CONCERN, State of North Carolina
DO NOT COLLECT: PROTECTED SPECIES

Midland Water Snake
Nerodia sipedon pleuralis

Pattern and/or color may be extremely variable throughout range.

DATE:

LOCATION:

HABITAT:

WEATHER:

SIZE/SEX:

REMARKS:

**Banded Water Snake,
Southern Banded
Water Snake**
Nerodia fasciata fasciata

Pattern and/or color may be extremely variable throughout range.

DATE:

LOCATION:

HABITAT:

WEATHER:

SIZE/SEX:

REMARKS:

**Florida Banded Water
Snake**
Nerodia fasciata pictiventris

Pattern and/or color may be extremely variable throughout range.

DATE:

LOCATION:

HABITAT:

WEATHER:

SIZE/SEX:

REMARKS:

Very dark, often nearly jet black individuals with little or no trace of dorsal pattern are commonly encountered in some portions of the range, especially in the Everglades region. In these snakes, even the wormlike belly pattern is usually black.

Florida Banded Water Snake (black phase)
Nerodia fasciata pictiventris

DATE:

LOCATION:

HABITAT:

WEATHER:

SIZE/SEX:

REMARKS:

Pattern and/or color may be extremely variable throughout range.

Broad-banded Water Snake
Nerodia fasciata confluens

DATE:

LOCATION:

STATUS: ENDANGERED, states of Kentucky and Illinois
DO NOT COLLECT: PROTECTED SPECIES

HABITAT:

WEATHER:

SIZE/SEX:

REMARKS:

DATE:

Gulf Salt Marsh Snake
Nerodia clarkii clarkii

LOCATION:

STATUS: CANDIDATE, Federal endangered or threatened species listing

HABITAT:

WEATHER:

SIZE/SEX:

REMARKS:

**Atlantic Salt
Marsh Snake**
Nerodia clarkii taeniata

STATUS: THREATENED,
Federal, State of Florida
**DO NOT COLLECT:
PROTECTED SPECIES**

DATE:

LOCATION:

HABITAT:

WEATHER:

SIZE/SEX:

REMARKS:

**Mangrove Salt Marsh
Snake (dark phase)**
*Nerodia clarkii
compressicauda*

DATE:

LOCATION:

HABITAT:

WEATHER:

SIZE/SEX:

REMARKS:

**Mangrove Salt Marsh
Snake (red/orange phase)**
*Nerodia clarkii
compressicauda*

DATE:

LOCATION:

HABITAT:

WEATHER:

SIZE/SEX:

REMARKS:

DATE:

LOCATION:

HABITAT:

WEATHER:

SIZE/SEX:

REMARKS:

**Brazos Water Snake,
Harter's Water Snake**
Nerodia harteri harteri

STATUS: THREATENED,
State of Texas
CANDIDATE, Federal en-
dangered or threatened
species listing
**DO NOT COLLECT:
PROTECTED SPECIES**

DATE:

LOCATION:

HABITAT:

WEATHER:

SIZE/SEX:

REMARKS:

Concho Water Snake
*Nerodia harteri
paucimaculata*

STATUS: ENDANGERED,
State of Texas
THREATENED, Federal
**DO NOT COLLECT:
PROTECTED SPECIES**

DATE:

LOCATION:

HABITAT:

WEATHER:

SIZE/SEX:

REMARKS:

**Additional species,
subspecies, and forms**

COMMON NAME:

SCIENTIFIC NAME:

COMMON NAME: DATE:

                               LOCATION:

SCIENTIFIC NAME: HABITAT:

                               WEATHER:

                               SIZE/SEX:

                               REMARKS:

COMMON NAME: DATE:

                               LOCATION:

SCIENTIFIC NAME: HABITAT:

                               WEATHER:

                               SIZE/SEX:

                               REMARKS:

COMMON NAME: DATE:

                               LOCATION:

SCIENTIFIC NAME: HABITAT:

                               WEATHER:

                               SIZE/SEX:

                               REMARKS:

QUEEN, CRAYFISH, KIRTLAND'S, AND SWAMP SNAKES

Family: Colubridae
Genera: *Regina, Clonophis,* and *Seminatrix*

BOTH CRAYFISH snakes (*Regina*) and Kirtland's snakes (*Clonophis*) were formerly regarded as water snakes in the genus *Nerodia* (formerly *Natrix*) but are now assigned to other genera. Crayfish snakes are generally more slender than water snakes but are equally aquatic. Their name refers to their favorite type of prey, crayfish. Crayfish snakes do not usually bask as water snakes do.

The Kirtland's snake (*Clonophis*) is much less inclined toward aquatic habitats than crayfish and swamp snakes and may be found on wooded hillsides, in meadows, marshes, and even city lots. Some authorities consider this genus to be closely related to the water snakes (*Nerodia*), while others believe it is more closely allied to the brown snakes (*Storeria*).

Black swamp snakes (*Seminatrix*) are small, very aquatic snakes restricted in distribution to the extreme southeastern United States. They are often found in floating mats of exotic water hyacinths.

DATE:

LOCATION:

HABITAT:

WEATHER:

SIZE/SEX:

REMARKS:

Queen Snake
Regina septemvittata septemvittata

STATUS: ENDANGERED, State of Wisconsin
WATCHLIST SPECIES, State of New York
DO NOT COLLECT: PROTECTED SPECIES

Mobile Queen Snake
Regina septemvittata mobila

No longer considered a distinct subspecies, this is a darker form with no dark dorsal stripe present. It is found along the Gulf Coast of southern Alabama (Mobile Bay) and extreme western Florida.

DATE:

LOCATION:

HABITAT:

WEATHER:

SIZE/SEX:

REMARKS:

Graham's Crayfish Snake
Regina grahamii grahamii

DATE:

LOCATION:

HABITAT:

WEATHER:

SIZE/SEX:

REMARKS:

Graham's Crayfish Snake (dark phase)
Regina grahamii grahamii

Individuals from some areas of Iowa are very dark, usually brown, with dorsal pattern or stripes very hard to distinguish.

DATE:

LOCATION:

HABITAT:

WEATHER:

SIZE/SEX:

REMARKS:

DATE:

LOCATION:

HABITAT:

WEATHER:

SIZE/SEX:

REMARKS:

Glossy Crayfish Snake
Regina rigida rigida

DATE:

LOCATION:

HABITAT:

WEATHER:

SIZE/SEX:

REMARKS:

Gulf Glossy Crayfish Snake
Regina rigida sinicola

STATUS: SPECIES OF SPECIAL CONCERN, State of Oklahoma
DO NOT COLLECT: PROTECTED SPECIES

DATE:

LOCATION:

HABITAT:

WEATHER:

SIZE/SEX:

REMARKS:

Delta Glossy Crayfish Snake
Regina rigida deltae

Striped Crayfish Snake
Regina alleni alleni

DATE:

LOCATION:

HABITAT:

WEATHER:

SIZE/SEX:

REMARKS:

Everglades Crayfish Snake
Regina alleni lineapiatus

This form differs from the Striped Crayfish Snake in that its belly has a distinct row of black spots or occasionally a dark median belly stripe. It is no longer considered a distinct subspecies.

DATE:

LOCATION:

HABITAT:

WEATHER:

SIZE/SEX:

REMARKS:

Kirtland's Snake
Clonophis kirtlandii

STATUS: ENDANGERED, states of Pennsylvania, Kentucky, and Michigan CANDIDATE, Federal endangered or threatened species listing
DO NOT COLLECT: PROTECTED SPECIES

DATE:

LOCATION:

HABITAT:

WEATHER:

SIZE/SEX:

REMARKS:

DATE:

LOCATION:

HABITAT:

WEATHER:

SIZE/SEX:

REMARKS:

North Florida Black Swamp Snake
Seminatrix pygaea pygaea

DATE:

LOCATION:

HABITAT:

WEATHER:

SIZE/SEX:

REMARKS:

South Florida Black Swamp Snake
Seminatrix pygaea cyclas

DATE:

LOCATION:

HABITAT:

WEATHER:

SIZE/SEX:

REMARKS:

Carolina Black Swamp Snake
Seminatrix pygaea paludis

Additional species, subspecies, and forms

COMMON NAME:

SCIENTIFIC NAME:

DATE:

LOCATION:

HABITAT:

WEATHER:

SIZE/SEX:

REMARKS:

COMMON NAME:

SCIENTIFIC NAME:

DATE:

LOCATION:

HABITAT:

WEATHER:

SIZE/SEX:

REMARKS:

COMMON NAME:

SCIENTIFIC NAME:

DATE:

LOCATION:

HABITAT:

WEATHER:

SIZE/SEX:

REMARKS:

COLOR PLATES

*References to text pages are indicated
in parentheses after species' scientific name.*

*All photographs by Chris Scott
unless otherwise indicated.*

Matthew Scott, son of the author,
holding an Eastern Kingsnake
Lampropeltis getulus getulus

Desert Kingsnake/
California Kingsnake

INTERGRADE
*Lampropeltis getulus
splendida/Lampropeltis
getulus californiae* (P.23)

DAN FISCHER

Western Blind Snake,
Southwestern Blind Snake
*Leptotyphlops humilis
humilis* (P.31)

R.D. BARTLETT

R.D. BARTLETT

Pacific Rubber Boa
Charina bottae bottae (P.35)

The "two-headed snake" using its tail as a decoy.

California Rosy Boa
DESERT PHASE
Lichanura trivirgata myriolepis (P.36)

Mexican Rosy Boa
Lichanura trivirgata trivirgata (P.37)

Brown Water Snake
Nerodia taxispilota (P.43)

Redbelly Water Snake
Nerodia erythrogaster erythrogaster (P.43)

R.D. BARTLETT

Florida Banded Water Snake
Nerodia fasciata pictiventris (P.46)

R.D. BARTLETT

R.D. BARTLETT

Mangrove Salt Marsh Snake
RED/ORANGE PHASE
Nerodia clarkii compressicauda (P.48)

R.D. BARTLETT

Queen Snake
Regina septemvittata septemvittata (P.51)

Western Blackneck Garter Snake
Thamnophis cyrtopsis cyrtopsis (P.65)

Narrow-headed Garter Snake
Thamnophis rufipunctatus
(P.66)

WALTER R. RICHARDSON

Hammond Two-striped Garter Snake
Thamnophis hammondi hammondi (P.70)

WALTER R. RICHARDSON

Peninsula Ribbon Snake, Southern Ribbon Snake
Thamnophis sauritus sackeni
(P.72)

R.D. BARTLETT

R.D. BARTLETT

Bluestripe Ribbon Snake
Thamnophis sauritus nitae
(P.72)

Florida Brown Snake
Storeria dekayi victa (P.79)

R.D. BARTLETT

R.D. BARTLETT

Northern Redbelly Snake
GRAY AND REDDISH BROWN PHASES
Storeria occipitomaculata
occipitomaculata (P.79)

Regal Ringneck Snake
Diadophis punctatus regalis
(P.85)

Northwestern Ringneck Snake
Diadophis punctatus occidentalis (P.86)

R.D. BARTLETT

Eastern Worm Snake
Carphophis amoenus amoenus (P.89)

R.D. BARTLETT

R.D. BARTLETT

Pine Woods Snake
Rhadinaea flavilata (P.88)

R.D. BARTLETT

Sharp-tail Snake
Contia tenuis (P.89)

Mexican Hognose Snake
Heterodon nasicus kennerlyi
(P.95)

Florida Scarlet Snake
ABBERRANT
*Cemophora coccinea
coccinea* (P.97)

R.D. BARTLETT

Texas Longnose Snake
*Rhinocheilus lecontei
tessellatus* (P.98)

Western Longnose Snake
DESERT OR CLARUS PHASE
Rhinocheilus lecontei lecontei
(P.98)

Ground Snake
PLAIN AND BANDED PHASES
Sonora semiannulata
(P.99, 100)

R.D. BARTLETT

Eastern Mud Snake
Farancia abacura abacura
(P.103)

Rough Green Snake
Opheodrys aestivus (P.106)

R.D. BARTLETT

Northern Black Racer
*Coluber constrictor
constrictor* (P.109)

Lined Coachwhip Snake
*Masticophis flagellum
lineatulus* (P.114)

DAN FISCHER

Red Coachwhip Snake
Masticophis flagellum piceus
(P.113)

Sonoran Whipsnake
Masticophis bilineatus bilineatus (P.118)

Plateau Patchnose Snake, Mountain Patchnose Snake
Salvadora grahamiae grahamiae (P.119)

Eastern Indigo Snake
Drymarchon corais couperi (P.123)

Black Pine Snake
JUVENILE
*Pituophis melanoleucus
lodingi* (P.127)

Sonoran Gopher Snake
*Pituophis melanoleucus
affinis* (P.128)

Great Basin Gopher Snake
*Pituophis melanoleucus
deserticola* (P.128)

San Diego Gopher Snake
Pituophis melanoleucus annectens (P.129)

Kansas Glossy Snake
Arizona elegans elegans (P.130)

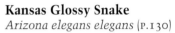

Painted Desert Glossy Snake
Arizona elegans philipi (P.130)

Eating a roadkill kangaroo rat.

Desert Glossy Snake
Arizona elegans eburnata
(P.131)

Corn Snake, Red Rat Snake
Elaphe guttata guttata (P.134)

Rosy Rat Snake
Elaphe guttata rosacea (P.135)

R.D. BARTLETT

Eastern Fox Snake
Elaphe vulpina gloydi (P.136)

R.D. BARTLETT

Gulf Hammock Rat Snake
Elaphe obsoleta williamsi
(P.138)

R.D. BARTLETT

Western Green Rat Snake
Senticolis triaspis intermedia
(P.139)

Trans-Pecos Rat Snake
Bogertophis subocularis
subocularis (P.140)

BLOND PHASE

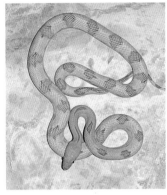

WALTER R. RICHARDSON

Mexican Black Kingsnake
Lampropeltis getulus nigritus
(P.146)

California Kingsnake

BANDED PHASE
Lampropeltis getulus
californiae (P.147)

Huachuca Mountain Kingsnake
Lampropeltis pyromelana woodini (P.150)

DAN FISCHER

Gray-banded Kingsnake
LIGHT ALTERNA PHASE
Lampropeltis alterna (P.153)

Gray-banded Kingsnake
DARK ALTERNA PHASE
Lampropeltis alterna (P.153)

Gray-banded Kingsnake

LIGHT BLAIR'S PHASE
Lampropeltis alterna (P.152)

Gray-banded Kingsnake

DARK BLAIR'S PHASE
Lampropeltis alterna (P.153)

ABERRANT DIAMONDBACK PHASE

Coastal Plain Milk Snake

Lampropeltis triangulum temporalis (P.154)

R.D. BARTLETT

Clouded Leafnose and Pima Saddled Leafnose Snakes
Phyllorhynchus decurtatus nubilis
Phyllorhynchus browni browni
(P.160)

Colorado Desert Shovelnose Snake
Chionactis occipitalis annulata (P.161)

ANZA-BORREGO PHASE (P.162)

WALTER R. RICHARDSON

Texas Night Snake
Hypsiglena torquata jani
(P.167)

Spotted Night Snake
Hypsiglena torquata
ochrorhyncha (P.167)

Brown Vine Snake
Oxybelis aeneus (P.168)

R.D. BARTLETT

Mexican Hooknose Snake
Ficimia streckeri (P.169)

Plains Blackhead Snake
Tantilla nigriceps nigriceps
(P.171)

R.D. BARTLETT

Texas Lyre Snake
Trimorphodon biscutatus vilkinsoni (P.175)

Southern Copperhead
Agkistrodon contortrix contortrix (P.182)

Trans-Pecos Copperhead
*Agkistrodon contortrix
pictigaster* (P.183)

Eastern Cottonmouth
LEUCISTIC
*Agkistrodon piscivorus
piscivorus* (P.184)

R.D. BARTLETT

Florida Cottonmouth
JUVENILE
*Agkistrodon piscivorus
conanti* (P.184)

R.D. BARTLETT

R.D. BARTLETT

Western Cottonmouth
Agkistrodon piscivorus leucostoma (P.184)

Western Diamondback Rattlesnake
REDDISH BROWN PHASE
Crotalus atrox (P.188)

Southwestern Speckled Rattlesnake
Crotalus mitchellii pyrrhus (P.189)

Banded Rock Rattlesnake
Crotalus lepidus klauberi
(P.190)

Mottled Rock Rattlesnake
Crotalus lepidus lepidus
(P.191)

Colorado Desert Sidewinder

JUVENILE
Crotalus cerastes laterorepens
(P.193)

**Northern Blacktail
Rattlesnake**
Crotalus molossus molossus
(P.193)

Tiger Rattlesnake
Crotalus tigris (P.194)

Mojave Rattlesnake
*Crotalus scutulatus
scutulatus* (P.194)

Arizona Black Rattlesnake
Crotalus viridis cerberus
(P.195)

Grand Canyon Rattlesnake
Crotalus viridis abyssus
(P.196)

Hopi Rattlesnake
Crotalus viridis nuntius
(P.197)

Timber Rattlesnake
JUVENILE LIGHT PHASE
Crotalus horridus horridus
(P.198)

Timber ("Canebrake") Rattlesnake
JUVENILE CANEBRAKE PHASE
Crotalus horridus atricaudatus
(P.199)

Western Twin-spotted Rattlesnake
Crotalus pricei pricei (P.200)

Arizona Ridgenose Rattlesnake
Crotalus willardi willardi
(P.200)

Animas Ridgenose Rattlesnake
Crotalus willardi obscurus
(P.200)

Desert Grassland Massassauga
Sistrurus catenatus edwardsi
(P.202)

Carolina Pigmy Rattlesnake
MATTAMUSKEET OR RED PHASE
Sistrurus miliarius miliarius
(P.202)

R.D. BARTLETT

R.D. BARTLETT

Eastern Coral Snake
Micrurus fulvius fulvius
(P.207)

Arizona Coral Snake
*Micruroides euryxanthus
euryxanthus* (P.208)

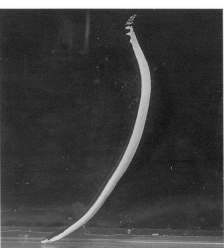

NEW YORK ZOOLOGICAL SOCIETY/© WILDLIFE CONSERVATION SOCIETY

Yellow-bellied Sea Snake
Pelamis platurus (P.210)

GARTER, RIBBON, AND LINED SNAKES

Family: Colubridae
Genera: *Thamnophis* and *Tropidoclonion*

OFTEN CALLED "garden snake," the garter snake is probably the best-known harmless snake found in the United States. These species are commonly kept as childhood pets. They are native to almost every state and are often the most abundant serpents throughout their range. The Common Garter Snake is found farther north than any other reptile in the Western Hemisphere.

Most garter snakes and ribbon snakes are small to moderate in size, slender, and usually striped longitudinally. Ribbon snakes are more slender than garter snakes. These genera are closely related to the water snakes (*Nerodia*), but unlike water snakes, garter snakes almost always have single anal plates. Also in common with water snakes, they are often found in aquatic or riparian habitats where they feed on frogs, toads, fish, and salamanders.

The lined snake, genus *Tropidoclonion*, is represented in the United States by a single species. There are four forms that are extremely hard to differentiate and not considered to be distinct subspecies by some herpetologists. The lined snake looks much like its close relative the garter snake, with which it shares similar habits and the same habitats. It is a small snake, rarely exceeding 18 inches in length.

**Eastern Garter Snake,
Common Garter Snake**
Thamnophis sirtalis sirtalis

Pattern and/or color may be extremely variable throughout range.

DATE:

LOCATION:

HABITAT:

WEATHER:

SIZE/SEX:

REMARKS:

**Eastern Garter Snake
(black phase)**
Thamnophis sirtalis sirtalis

Melanistic Eastern Garter Snakes are commonly encountered in southern Ontario, on the north central shore of Lake Erie. Many of these are nearly jet black in color.

DATE:

LOCATION:

HABITAT:

WEATHER:

SIZE/SEX:

REMARKS:

Maritime Garter Snake
*Thamnophis sirtalis
pallidula*

DATE:

LOCATION:

HABITAT:

WEATHER:

SIZE/SEX:

REMARKS:

DATE:

LOCATION:

HABITAT:

WEATHER:

SIZE/SEX:

REMARKS:

Chicago Garter Snake
*Thamnophis sirtalis
semifasciatus*

DATE:

LOCATION:

HABITAT:

WEATHER:

SIZE/SEX:

REMARKS:

Red-sided Garter Snake
*Thamnophis sirtalis
parietalis*

Very dark, nearly black individuals occur in several locations in central Montana.

DATE:

LOCATION:

HABITAT:

WEATHER:

SIZE/SEX:

REMARKS:

**Red-sided Garter Snake
(dark phase)**
*Thamnophis sirtalis
parietalis*

New Mexico Garter Snake
Thamnophis sirtalis dorsalis

DATE:

LOCATION:

HABITAT:

WEATHER:

SIZE/SEX:

REMARKS:

Texas Garter Snake
Thamnophis sirtalis annectens

STATUS: CANDIDATE, Federal endangered or threatened species listing CANDIDATE, State of Oklahoma

DATE:

LOCATION:

HABITAT:

WEATHER:

SIZE/SEX:

REMARKS:

Bluestripe Garter Snake
Thamnophis sirtalis similis

DATE:

LOCATION:

HABITAT:

WEATHER:

SIZE/SEX:

REMARKS:

DATE:

LOCATION:

HABITAT:

WEATHER:

SIZE/SEX:

REMARKS:

Red-spotted Garter Snake
Thamnophis sirtalis concinnus

DATE:

LOCATION:

HABITAT:

WEATHER:

SIZE/SEX:

REMARKS:

Puget Sound Garter Snake
Thamnophis sirtalis pickeringi

DATE:

LOCATION:

HABITAT:

WEATHER:

SIZE/SEX:

REMARKS:

Valley Garter Snake
Thamnophis sirtalis fitchi

**Valley Garter Snake
(gray phase)**
Thamnophis sirtalis fitchi

Slate gray individuals occur at Crater Lake, Oregon.

DATE:

LOCATION:

HABITAT:

WEATHER:

SIZE/SEX:

REMARKS:

**San Francisco Garter
Snake**
*Thamnophis sirtalis
tetrataenia*

STATUS: ENDANGERED,
Federal, State of
California
**DO NOT COLLECT:
PROTECTED SPECIES**

DATE:

LOCATION:

HABITAT:

WEATHER:

SIZE/SEX:

REMARKS:

**California Red-sided
Garter Snake**
*Thamnophis sirtalis
infernalis*

DATE:

LOCATION:

HABITAT:

WEATHER:

SIZE/SEX:

REMARKS:

Pattern and/or color may be extremely variable throughout range.

DATE:

LOCATION:

HABITAT:

WEATHER:

SIZE/SEX:

REMARKS:

Eastern Plains Garter Snake
Thamnophis radix radix

STATUS: ENDANGERED, State of Ohio
DO NOT COLLECT: PROTECTED SPECIES

Pattern and/or color may be extremely variable throughout range.

DATE:

LOCATION:

HABITAT:

WEATHER:

SIZE/SEX:

REMARKS:

Western Plains Garter Snake
Thamnophis radix haydenii

Pattern and/or color may be extremely variable throughout range.

DATE:

LOCATION:

HABITAT:

WEATHER:

SIZE/SEX:

REMARKS:

Butler's Garter Snake
Thamnophis butleri

STATUS: THREATENED, State of Indiana
DO NOT COLLECT: PROTECTED SPECIES

Shorthead Garter Snake
Thamnophis brachystoma

STATUS: CANDIDATE,
Federal endangered or
threatened species listing
WATCHLIST SPECIES:
State of New York

DATE:

LOCATION:

HABITAT:

WEATHER:

SIZE/SEX:

REMARKS:

**Eastern Checkered Garter
Snake**
*Thamnophis marcianus
marcianus*

STATUS: THREATENED,
State of Kansas
**DO NOT COLLECT:
PROTECTED SPECIES**

DATE:

LOCATION:

HABITAT:

WEATHER:

SIZE/SEX:

REMARKS:

**Western Checkered
Garter Snake**
*Thamnophis marcianus
nigrolateris*

STATUS: THREATENED,
State of Kansas
**DO NOT COLLECT:
PROTECTED SPECIES**

Color may be somewhat variable throughout range. This species
is not widely recognized as a distinct subspecies. According to
Robert C. Stebbins (*Western Reptiles and Amphibians*): "This
snake is rapidly disappearing on major river systems of S. Arizona,
New Mexico, and adjacent Mexico."

DATE:

LOCATION:

HABITAT:

WEATHER:

SIZE/SEX:

REMARKS:

Pattern and/or color may be extremely variable throughout range.

DATE:

LOCATION:

HABITAT:

WEATHER:

SIZE/SEX:

REMARKS:

Western Blackneck Garter Snake
Thamnophis cyrtopsis cyrtopsis

Individuals from the Big Bend area of Texas are usually very dark, often black, in color.

DATE:

LOCATION:

HABITAT:

WEATHER:

SIZE/SEX:

REMARKS:

Western Blackneck Garter Snake (Big Bend phase)
Thamnophis cyrtopsis cyrtopsis

DATE:

LOCATION:

HABITAT:

WEATHER:

SIZE/SEX:

REMARKS:

Eastern Blackneck Garter Snake
Thamnophis cyrtopsis ocellatus

Narrow-headed Garter Snake
Thamnophis rufipunctatus

STATUS: ENDANGERED, State of New Mexico, Group 2
CANDIDATE, endangered or threatened species listing, State of Arizona
DO NOT COLLECT: PROTECTED SPECIES

DATE:

LOCATION:

HABITAT:

WEATHER:

SIZE/SEX:

REMARKS:

Mountain Garter Snake
Thamnophis elegans elegans

Color may be somewhat variable throughout range.

DATE:

LOCATION:

HABITAT:

WEATHER:

SIZE/SEX:

REMARKS:

Wandering Garter Snake
Thamnophis elegans vagrans

Pattern and/or color may be somewhat variable throughout range.

DATE:

LOCATION:

HABITAT:

WEATHER:

SIZE/SEX:

REMARKS:

Very dark, nearly black individuals have been found in the Puget Sound, Washington, area and in eastern Oregon.

Wandering Garter Snake (black phase)
Thamnophis elegans vagrans

DATE:

LOCATION:

HABITAT:

WEATHER:

SIZE/SEX:

REMARKS:

Pattern and/or color may be extremely variable throughout range.

Coast Garter Snake
Thamnophis elegans terrestris

DATE:

LOCATION:

HABITAT:

WEATHER:

SIZE/SEX:

REMARKS:

This phase occurs in the Santa Cruz Mountains, California.

Coast Garter Snake (dark phase)
Thamnophis elegans terrestris

DATE:

LOCATION:

HABITAT:

WEATHER:

SIZE/SEX:

REMARKS:

Klamath Garter Snake   DATE:

Thamnophis elegans
biscutatus   LOCATION:

                              HABITAT:

                              WEATHER:

                              SIZE/SEX:

                              REMARKS:

Oregon Garter Snake   DATE:

Thamnophis couchi
hydrophilus   LOCATION:

                              HABITAT:

                              WEATHER:

                              SIZE/SEX:

                              REMARKS:

Sierra Garter Snake   DATE:

Thamnophis couchi couchi   LOCATION:

                              HABITAT:

                              WEATHER:

                              SIZE/SEX:

                              REMARKS:

DATE:

LOCATION:

HABITAT:

WEATHER:

SIZE/SEX:

REMARKS:

Giant Garter Snake
Thamnophis couchi gigas

STATUS: ENDANGERED,
State of California
CANDIDATE, Federal
endangered threatened
species listing
**DO NOT COLLECT:
PROTECTED SPECIES**

DATE:

LOCATION:

HABITAT:

WEATHER:

SIZE/SEX:

REMARKS:

Aquatic Garter Snake
*Thamnophis couchi
aquaticus*

Pattern and/or color may be extremely variable throughout range.

DATE:

LOCATION:

HABITAT:

WEATHER:

SIZE/SEX:

REMARKS:

Santa Cruz Garter Snake
Thamnophis couchi atratus

**Hammond Two-striped
Garter Snake**
*Thamnophis hammondi
hammondi*

STATUS: CANDIDATE,
Federal endangered or
threatened species listing

DATE:

LOCATION:

HABITAT:

WEATHER:

SIZE/SEX:

REMARKS:

**Hammond Two-striped
Garter Snake
(black phase)**
*Thamnophis hammondi
hammondi*

STATUS: CANDIDATE,
Federal endangered or
threatened species listing

Very dark, nearly black individuals occur on the California Coast
from Monterey County south to San Luis Obispo County.

DATE:

LOCATION:

HABITAT:

WEATHER:

SIZE/SEX:

REMARKS:

**Northwestern Garter
Snake**
Thamnophis ordinoides

Pattern and/or color may be extremely variable throughout range.

DATE:

LOCATION:

HABITAT:

WEATHER:

SIZE/SEX:

REMARKS:

DATE:

LOCATION:

HABITAT:

WEATHER:

SIZE/SEX:

REMARKS:

Mexican Garter Snake
*Thamnophis eques
megalops*

STATUS: ENDANGERED,
State of New Mexico,
Group 1
CANDIDATE, Federal,
State of Arizona endan-
gered or threatened spe-
cies listing
**DO NOT COLLECT:
PROTECTED SPECIES**

DATE:

LOCATION:

HABITAT:

WEATHER:

SIZE/SEX:

REMARKS:

Eastern Ribbon Snake
*Thamnophis sauritus
sauritus*

STATUS: ENDANGERED,
State of Illinois
SPECIES OF SPECIAL
CONCERN, states of
Connecticut, Kentucky,
and Maine
**DO NOT COLLECT:
PROTECTED SPECIES**

DATE:

LOCATION:

HABITAT:

WEATHER:

SIZE/SEX:

REMARKS:

Northern Ribbon Snake
*Thamnophis sauritus
septentrionalis*

STATUS: ENDANGERED,
State of Wisconsin
SPECIES OF SPECIAL
CONCERN, State of
Maine
**DO NOT COLLECT:
PROTECTED SPECIES**

Peninsula Ribbon Snake, Southern Ribbon Snake
Thamnophis sauritus sackenii

STATUS: THREATENED, State of Florida (Lower Keys population only)
DO NOT COLLECT: PROTECTED SPECIES

DATE:

LOCATION:

HABITAT:

WEATHER:

SIZE/SEX:

REMARKS:

Lower Keys Ribbon Snake
Thamnophis sauritus sackenii

STATUS: THREATENED, State of Florida (Lower Keys population only)
DO NOT COLLECT: PROTECTED SPECIES

This color morph of the Peninsula Ribbon Snake has a bright orange or yellow middorsal stripe bordered by thin black stripes on each side.

DATE:

LOCATION:

HABITAT:

WEATHER:

SIZE/SEX:

REMARKS:

Bluestripe Ribbon Snake
Thamnophis sauritus nitae

This form and the Bluestripe Garter Snake (*Thamnophis sirtalis similis*) are restricted in range to the "Gulf Hammock" region of northwestern Florida.

DATE:

LOCATION:

HABITAT:

WEATHER:

SIZE/SEX:

REMARKS:

DATE:

LOCATION:

HABITAT:

WEATHER:

SIZE/SEX:

REMARKS:

Western Ribbon Snake
Thamnophis proximus proximus

STATUS: ENDANGERED, states of Wisconsin and New Mexico, Group 2 SPECIES OF SPECIAL CONCERN, State of Indiana
DO NOT COLLECT: PROTECTED SPECIES

DATE:

LOCATION:

HABITAT:

WEATHER:

SIZE/SEX:

REMARKS:

Gulf Coast Ribbon Snake
Thamnophis proximus orarius

DATE:

LOCATION:

HABITAT:

WEATHER:

SIZE/SEX:

REMARKS:

Arid Land Ribbon Snake
Thamnophis proximus diabolicus

Redstripe Ribbon Snake
Thamnophis proximus rubrilineatus

DATE:

LOCATION:

HABITAT:

WEATHER:

SIZE/SEX:

REMARKS:

Northern Lined Snake
Tropidoclonion lineatum lineatum

STATUS: THREATENED, State of South Dakota SPECIES OF SPECIAL CONCERN, State of Minnesota
DO NOT COLLECT: PROTECTED SPECIES

DATE:

LOCATION:

HABITAT:

WEATHER:

SIZE/SEX:

REMARKS:

Central Lined Snake
Tropidoclonion lineatum annectens

DATE:

LOCATION:

HABITAT:

WEATHER:

SIZE/SEX:

REMARKS:

DATE:

LOCATION:

HABITAT:

WEATHER:

SIZE/SEX:

REMARKS:

New Mexico Lined Snake
Tropidoclonion lineatum mertensi

DATE:

LOCATION:

HABITAT:

WEATHER:

SIZE/SEX:

REMARKS:

Texas Lined Snake
Tropidoclonion lineatum texanum

DATE:

LOCATION:

HABITAT:

WEATHER:

SIZE/SEX:

REMARKS:

Additional species, subspecies, and forms

COMMON NAME:

SCIENTIFIC NAME:

COMMON NAME: DATE:

                               LOCATION:

SCIENTIFIC NAME: HABITAT:

                               WEATHER:

                               SIZE/SEX:

                               REMARKS:

COMMON NAME: DATE:

                               LOCATION:

SCIENTIFIC NAME: HABITAT:

                               WEATHER:

                               SIZE/SEX:

                               REMARKS:

COMMON NAME: DATE:

                               LOCATION:

SCIENTIFIC NAME: HABITAT:

                               WEATHER:

                               SIZE/SEX:

                               REMARKS:

BROWN AND REDBELLY SNAKES

Family: Colubridae
Genus: *Storeria*

THESE SMALL snakes are related to the garter snakes (*Thamnophis*) and are found in the eastern and midwestern United States. They are secretive in nature and usually remain concealed beneath cover in moist areas. Brown snakes, particularly the Northern Brown Snake, often live near human habitation in city parks, dumps, vacant lots, etc., but due to their stealthy nature, they are rarely noticed. Redbelly snakes are usually found in more rural environments. Both generally feed on earthworms, salamanders, and slugs. Adults average 9 to 13 inches in length.

Pattern and/or color may be extremely variable throughout range.

DATE:

LOCATION:

HABITAT:

WEATHER:

SIZE/SEX:

REMARKS:

Northern Brown Snake
Storeria dekayi dekayi

STATUS: CANDIDATE, endangered or threatened species listing, State of Maine

Midland Brown Snake
Storeria dekayi wrightorum

Pattern and/or color may be extremely variable throughout range.

DATE:

LOCATION:

HABITAT:

WEATHER:

SIZE/SEX:

REMARKS:

Texas Brown Snake
Storeria dekayi texana

Pattern and/or color may be extremely variable throughout range.

DATE:

LOCATION:

HABITAT:

WEATHER:

SIZE/SEX:

REMARKS:

Marsh Brown Snake
Storeria dekayi limnetes

Pattern and/or color may be extremely variable throughout range.

DATE:

LOCATION:

HABITAT:

WEATHER:

SIZE/SEX:

REMARKS:

Pattern and/or color may be extremely variable throughout range.

Florida Brown Snake
Storeria dekayi victa

DATE:

LOCATION:

HABITAT:

WEATHER:

SIZE/SEX:

REMARKS:

STATUS: THREATENED, State of Florida (Lower Keys population)
DO NOT COLLECT: PROTECTED SPECIES

DATE:

LOCATION:

HABITAT:

WEATHER:

SIZE/SEX:

REMARKS:

Northern Redbelly Snake (reddish brown phase)
Storeria occipitomaculata occipitomaculata

STATUS: THREATENED, states of Kansas and South Dakota
DO NOT COLLECT: PROTECTED SPECIES

DATE:

LOCATION:

HABITAT:

WEATHER:

SIZE/SEX:

REMARKS:

Northern Redbelly Snake (gray phase)
Storeria occipitomaculata occipitomaculata

STATUS: THREATENED, states of Kansas and South Dakota
DO NOT COLLECT: PROTECTED SPECIES

Florida Redbelly Snake
Storeria occipitomaculata obscura

Pattern and/or color may be extremely variable throughout range.

DATE:

LOCATION:

HABITAT:

WEATHER:

SIZE/SEX:

REMARKS:

Black Hills Redbelly Snake (gray phase)
Storeria occipitomaculata pahasapae

STATUS: CANDIDATE, Federal endangered or threatened species listing

DATE:

LOCATION:

HABITAT:

WEATHER:

SIZE/SEX:

REMARKS:

Black Hills Redbelly Snake (reddish phase)
Storeria occipitomaculata pahasapae

STATUS: CANDIDATE, Federal endangered or threatened species listing

DATE:

LOCATION:

HABITAT:

WEATHER:

SIZE/SEX:

REMARKS:

DATE:

LOCATION:

HABITAT:

WEATHER:

SIZE/SEX:

REMARKS:

**Additional species,
subspecies, and forms**

COMMON NAME:

SCIENTIFIC NAME:

DATE:

LOCATION:

HABITAT:

WEATHER:

SIZE/SEX:

REMARKS:

COMMON NAME:

SCIENTIFIC NAME:

DATE:

LOCATION:

HABITAT:

WEATHER:

SIZE/SEX:

REMARKS:

COMMON NAME:

SCIENTIFIC NAME:

SMALL WOODLAND SNAKES
Ringneck, Worm, Pine Woods, Sharp-tail, and Earth Snakes

Family: Colubridae
Genera: *Diadophis, Carphophis, Rhadinaea, Contia,* and *Virginia*

THESE SNAKES are secretive in nature and adept at remaining concealed under rocks, the bark of fallen trees, and other cover much of the time. Ringnecks of several species range from coast to coast, but in the West they are local in distribution and are usually restricted to mountainous areas and the banks of water courses in arid habitats. Ringnecks from western and certain southern populations have a tendency to twist their tails when alarmed, displaying to a potential predator the bright red undersurface, which is often interpreted as a "danger" signal. Interestingly, Northern and most Southern ringnecks, which do not have the bright red underside, do not exhibit this behavior. Ringneck snakes average 10 to 15 inches in length, while the Regal Ringneck occasionally exceeds 30 inches.

Worm snakes (*Carphophis*) average 7 to 11 inches in length, and pine woods snakes average only slightly larger at 10 to 13 inches. Worm snakes and pine woods snakes (*Rhadinaea*) are partial to sandy soils and are usually found in wooded areas where they feed on earthworms and insect larvae. Pine woods snakes also feed on lizards and amphibians. When handled, the worm snake often presses the pointed tip of its tail into one's hand.

Earth snakes (*Virginia*) are slightly smaller than worm snakes and are often found in the same habitat. I have found Smooth Earth Snakes and Eastern Worm Snakes under the same board. Worm snakes, earth snakes, and pine woods snakes are restricted to the eastern United States. Sharp-tail snakes (*Contia*), however, are found only in the western United States, usually in moist habitats that range from pastures to woodland areas. Slugs make up the greater part of their diet.

DATE: **Northern Ringneck Snake**
                                                                  Diadophis punctatus
LOCATION: *edwardsi*

HABITAT:

WEATHER:

SIZE/SEX:

REMARKS:

DATE: **Southern Ringneck Snake**
                                                                  Diadophis punctatus
LOCATION: *punctatus*

HABITAT:

WEATHER:

SIZE/SEX:

REMARKS:

Unlike the typical Southern Ringneck, snakes from peninsula   **Southern Ringneck Snake**
Florida often display a brilliant red towards the tip of the under- **(peninsula Florida phase)**
side of the tail. This form becomes more common as one travels   *Diadophis punctatus*
south in Florida.   *punctatus*

DATE:

LOCATION:

HABITAT:

WEATHER:

SIZE/SEX:

REMARKS:

Key Ringneck Snake
Diadophis punctatus acricus

STATUS: THREATENED, State of Florida
CANDIDATE, Federal endangered or threatened species listing
DO NOT COLLECT: PROTECTED SPECIES

DATE:

LOCATION:

HABITAT:

WEATHER:

SIZE/SEX:

REMARKS:

Mississippi Ringneck Snake
Diadophis punctatus stictogenys

DATE:

LOCATION:

HABITAT:

WEATHER:

SIZE/SEX:

REMARKS:

Prairie Ringneck Snake
Diadophis punctatus arnyi

DATE:

LOCATION:

HABITAT:

WEATHER:

SIZE/SEX:

REMARKS:

Pattern and/or color may be extremely variable throughout range.

DATE:

LOCATION:

HABITAT:

WEATHER:

SIZE/SEX:

REMARKS:

Regal Ringneck Snake
Diadophis punctatus regalis

STATUS: SPECIES OF SPE-
CIAL CONCERN, State
of Idaho, Category C
**DO NOT COLLECT:
PROTECTED SPECIES**

In several populations from Utah, Arizona, and southern New
Mexico, the neck band is absent.

DATE:

LOCATION:

HABITAT:

WEATHER:

SIZE/SEX:

REMARKS:

**Regal Ringneck Snake
(bandless phase)**
Diadophis punctatus regalis

STATUS: SPECIES OF SPE-
CIAL CONCERN, State
of Idaho, Category C
**DO NOT COLLECT:
PROTECTED SPECIES**

DATE:

LOCATION:

HABITAT:

WEATHER:

SIZE/SEX:

REMARKS:

Pacific Ringneck Snake
*Diadophis punctatus
amabilis*

San Bernardino Ringneck Snake
Diadophis punctatus modestus

STATUS: CANDIDATE, Federal endangered or threatened species listing

DATE:

LOCATION:

HABITAT:

WEATHER:

SIZE/SEX:

REMARKS:

Northwestern Ringneck Snake
Diadophis punctatus occidentalis

STATUS: SPECIES OF SPECIAL CONCERN, State of Idaho, Category C
DO NOT COLLECT: PROTECTED SPECIES

DATE:

LOCATION:

HABITAT:

WEATHER:

SIZE/SEX:

REMARKS:

Coral-bellied Ringneck Snake
Diadophis punctatus pulchellus

DATE:

LOCATION:

HABITAT:

WEATHER:

SIZE/SEX:

REMARKS:

DATE:

LOCATION:

HABITAT:

WEATHER:

SIZE/SEX:

REMARKS:

San Diego Ringneck Snake
Diadophis punctatus similis

STATUS: CANDIDATE, Federal endangered or threatened species listing

---

DATE:

LOCATION:

HABITAT:

WEATHER:

SIZE/SEX:

REMARKS:

Monterey Ringneck Snake
Diadophis punctatus vandenburghi

DATE:

LOCATION:

HABITAT:

WEATHER:

SIZE/SEX:

REMARKS:

Eastern Worm Snake
Carphophis amoenus amoenus

STATUS: THREATENED, State of Massachusetts SPECIES OF SPECIAL CONCERN, State of New York
DO NOT COLLECT: PROTECTED SPECIES

Midwest Worm Snake

Carphophis amoenus helenae

DATE:

LOCATION:

HABITAT:

WEATHER:

SIZE/SEX:

REMARKS:

Western Worm Snake

Carphophis vermis

STATUS: Considered IM-PERILED in Wisconsin and vulnerable to extirpation from this state.

DATE:

LOCATION:

HABITAT:

WEATHER:

SIZE/SEX:

REMARKS:

Pine Woods Snake

Rhadinaea flavilata

STATUS: ENDANGERED, State of Louisiana (Considered imperiled and very vulnerable to extirpation.)
DO NOT COLLECT: PROTECTED SPECIES

DATE:

LOCATION:

HABITAT:

WEATHER:

SIZE/SEX:

REMARKS:

DATE:

LOCATION:

HABITAT:

WEATHER:

SIZE/SEX:

REMARKS:

Sharp-tail Snake
Contia tenuis

STATUS: CANDIDATE, endangered or threatened species listing, State of Oregon

---

DATE:

LOCATION:

HABITAT:

WEATHER:

SIZE/SEX:

REMARKS:

Eastern Smooth Earth Snake
Virginia valeriae valeriae

STATUS: THREATENED, State of Massachusetts SPECIES OF SPECIAL CONCERN, State of New York
DO NOT COLLECT: PROTECTED SPECIES

DATE:

LOCATION:

HABITAT:

WEATHER:

SIZE/SEX:

REMARKS:

Mountain Smooth Earth Snake
Virginia valeriae pulchra

STATUS: ENDANGERED, State of Maryland SPECIES OF SPECIAL CONCERN, State of Virginia
DO NOT COLLECT: PROTECTED SPECIES

Western Smooth Earth Snake
Virginia valeriae elegans

STATUS: THREATENED, states of Kansas and Iowa
DO NOT COLLECT: PROTECTED SPECIES

DATE:

LOCATION:

HABITAT:

WEATHER:

SIZE/SEX:

REMARKS:

Rough Earth Snake
Virginia striatula

DATE:

LOCATION:

HABITAT:

WEATHER:

SIZE/SEX:

REMARKS:

Additional species, subspecies, and forms

COMMON NAME:

SCIENTIFIC NAME:

DATE:

LOCATION:

HABITAT:

WEATHER:

SIZE/SEX:

REMARKS:

DATE: COMMON NAME:

LOCATION:

HABITAT: SCIENTIFIC NAME:

WEATHER:

SIZE/SEX:

REMARKS:

DATE: COMMON NAME:

LOCATION:

HABITAT: SCIENTIFIC NAME:

WEATHER:

SIZE/SEX:

REMARKS:

DATE: COMMON NAME:

LOCATION:

HABITAT: SCIENTIFIC NAME:

WEATHER:

SIZE/SEX:

REMARKS:

HOGNOSE SNAKES

Family: Colubridae
Genus: *Heterodon*

THESE SMALL- to medium-sized, stout-bodied snakes exhibit perhaps the most unusual and surely the most amusing behavior of any of the American snakes. A member of this genus may put on a show of hostility that often begins by spreading its hood and inflating its body with air while hissing loudly and striking repeatedly (usually without even opening its mouth). This behavior mimics the actions of a cobra in an attempt to scare off an adversary. If the cobra impression is not successful, the hognose may throw itself into violent convulsions, roll over on its back, open its mouth, and play dead. If turned right side up, the snake will immediately roll over again and repeat this act. Western forms of the genus are less prone to this behavior than the Eastern Hognose Snake (*Heterodon platirhinos platirhinos*).

Because of these unusual habits, the hognose snake has received a bad reputation and is feared by many who call it a "Spreading Adder" or "Puff Adder." The hognose, however, is one of the most mild-mannered snakes, and these exhibitions are simply defensive bluffs designed by Mother Nature. This snake is found only in North America, nearly always in sandy habitats where it feeds on toads, its principal food. The upturned snout is used to dig for toads and also to burrow. Enlarged teeth on the rear upper jaw are believed to inject a mild venom into prey. Hognose snakes are harmless to humans.

DATE:

LOCATION:

HABITAT:

WEATHER:

SIZE/SEX:

REMARKS:

Eastern Hognose Snake
Heterodon platirhinos platirhinos

STATUS: THREATENED, State of South Dakota SPECIES OF SPECIAL CONCERN, states of Connecticut and New York
DO NOT COLLECT: PROTECTED SPECIES

Melanistic Eastern Hognose Snakes are not uncommon. Although they are usually found in the mountains of New York, New Jersey, and Connecticut, they may be encountered virtually anywhere in the species range.

DATE:

LOCATION:

HABITAT:

WEATHER:

SIZE/SEX:

REMARKS:

Eastern Hognose Snake, Black Hognose Snake (black phase)
Heterodon platirhinos platirhinos

STATUS: THREATENED, State of South Dakota SPECIES OF SPECIAL CONCERN, states of Connecticut and New York
DO NOT COLLECT: PROTECTED SPECIES

This morph is no longer considered a distinct subspecies. It is similar to the typical Eastern Hognose Snake; however, this form lacks the azygous shield between the internasals and prefrontals. This is a problematical form at best, reported only from eastern Dade County, Florida.

DATE:

LOCATION:

HABITAT:

WEATHER:

SIZE/SEX:

REMARKS:

Brown's Hognose Snake, South Florida Hognose Snake
Heterodon platirhinos browni

Southern Hognose Snake   DATE:
Heterodon simus
                                    LOCATION:
STATUS: ENDANGERED,
State of Mississippi   HABITAT:
CANDIDATE, Federal en-
                                    WEATHER:
dangered or threatened
species listing   SIZE/SEX:
DO NOT COLLECT:
                                    REMARKS:
PROTECTED SPECIES

Dusty Hognose Snake   DATE:
Heterodon nasicus gloydi
                                    LOCATION:
STATUS: ENDANGERED,
State of Iowa   HABITAT:
THREATENED, State of   WEATHER:
Illinois
RARE AND DECLIN-   SIZE/SEX:
ING, State of Missouri
                                    REMARKS:
DO NOT COLLECT:
PROTECTED SPECIES

Plains Hognose Snake   DATE:
Heterodon nasicus nasicus
                                    LOCATION:
STATUS: ENDANGERED,
State of Iowa   HABITAT:
THREATENED, State of   WEATHER:
Illinois
RARE AND DECLIN-   SIZE/SEX:
ING, State of Missouri
                                    REMARKS:
DO NOT COLLECT:
PROTECTED SPECIES

DATE:

LOCATION:

HABITAT:

WEATHER:

SIZE/SEX:

REMARKS:

Mexican Hognose Snake
Heterodon nasicus kennerlyi

DATE:

LOCATION:

HABITAT:

WEATHER:

SIZE/SEX:

REMARKS:

Additional species, subspecies, and forms

COMMON NAME:

SCIENTIFIC NAME:

DATE:

LOCATION:

HABITAT:

WEATHER:

SIZE/SEX:

REMARKS:

COMMON NAME:

SCIENTIFIC NAME:

SCARLET, LONGNOSE, SHORT-TAILED, AND GROUND SNAKES

Family: Colubridae
Genera: *Cemophora, Rhinocheilus, Stilosoma,* and *Sonora*

SNAKES FROM all four of these genera are usually subterranean burrowers, venturing up to the surface only at night or after heavy rains. Scarlet, longnose, and short-tailed snakes (*Cemophora, Rhinocheilus,* and *Stilosoma*) are believed to be related to kingsnakes and milksnakes (*Lampropeltis*), and are often similar in appearance and habits. Ground snakes (*Sonora*) are masters of disguise, and individuals show a great deal of variation in pattern and color. At one time the ground snakes were divided into two species and six or seven subspecies. It is now generally believed that there is but one species, with several very different color phases. The Ground Snake and the Gray-banded Kingsnake (*Lampropeltis alterna*) rank as the two most variable species of snakes in the United States. These snakes are often confused with other small species, including shovel-nosed (*Chionactis*) and banded sand snakes (*Chilomeniscus*). Scarlet snakes and, to a lesser extent, longnose snakes bear an unfortunate resemblance to the venomous coral snakes (*Micrurus* and *Micruroides*), and are often killed on sight for this reason.

All four genera are small- to medium-sized, with ground snakes averaging less than 12 inches in length, short-tailed, scarlet snakes rarely exceeding 22 inches, and longnose snakes occasionally exceeding 3 feet.

DATE:

LOCATION:

HABITAT:

WEATHER:

SIZE/SEX:

REMARKS:

Northern Scarlet Snake
Cemophora coccinea copei

STATUS: THREATENED, states of Texas and Indiana
SPECIES OF SPECIAL CONCERN, states of Oklahoma and Maryland (classified as a watch list species)
RARE AND DECLINING, State of Missouri
DO NOT COLLECT: PROTECTED SPECIES

DATE:

LOCATION:

HABITAT:

WEATHER:

SIZE/SEX:

REMARKS:

Florida Scarlet Snake
Cemophora coccinea coccinea

DATE:

LOCATION:

HABITAT:

WEATHER:

SIZE/SEX:

REMARKS:

Texas Scarlet Snake
Cemophora coccinea lineri

STATUS: THREATENED, State of Texas
DO NOT COLLECT: PROTECTED SPECIES

Texas Longnose Snake
Rhinocheilus lecontei
tessellatus

STATUS: THREATENED,
State of Kansas
SPECIES OF SPECIAL
CONCERN, State of
Oklahoma
DO NOT COLLECT:
PROTECTED SPECIES

DATE:

LOCATION:

HABITAT:

WEATHER:

SIZE/SEX:

REMARKS:

Western Longnose Snake
Rhinocheilus lecontei
lecontei

STATUS: SPECIES OF SPE-
CIAL CONCERN, State
of Idaho, Category B
DO NOT COLLECT:
PROTECTED SPECIES

DATE:

LOCATION:

HABITAT:

WEATHER:

SIZE/SEX:

REMARKS:

Western Longnose Snake
(desert or *clarus* phase)
Rhinocheilus lecontei
lecontei

Formerly considered a distinct subspecies, this form lacks all or most of the red coloration present in the typical Western Long-nose and may superficially resemble a California Kingsnake (*Lampropeltis getulus californiae*). It is most commonly encountered in the low Sonoran Desert.

DATE:

LOCATION:

HABITAT:

WEATHER:

SIZE/SEX:

REMARKS:

Distinguishing the two subspecies of short-tails requires some knowledge of morphology, as they are identical in appearance. The Eastern Short-tailed usually has six lower labials and the prefrontals are fused with the internasals. This subspecies is found from Putnam County south into Polk County, Florida.

Eastern Short-tailed Snake
Stilosoma extenuatum extenuatum

STATUS: THREATENED, State of Florida CANDIDATE, Federal endangered or threatened species listing
DO NOT COLLECT: PROTECTED SPECIES

DATE:

LOCATION:

HABITAT:

WEATHER:

SIZE/SEX:

REMARKS:

This subspecies usually has seven lower labials; the prefrontals and internasals are separate. The Western Short-tailed is found from Alachua County south into Pinellas County, Florida.

Western Short-tailed Snake
Stilosoma extenuatum arenicolor

STATUS: THREATENED, State of Florida CANDIDATE, Federal endangered or threatened species listing
DO NOT COLLECT: PROTECTED SPECIES

DATE:

LOCATION:

HABITAT:

WEATHER:

SIZE/SEX:

REMARKS:

DATE:

LOCATION:

HABITAT:

WEATHER:

SIZE/SEX:

REMARKS:

Ground Snake (plain phase)
Sonora semiannulata

STATUS: SPECIES OF SPECIAL CONCERN, State of Idaho, Category B
DO NOT COLLECT: PROTECTED SPECIES

**Ground Snake
(striped phase)**
Sonora semiannulata

STATUS: SPECIES OF SPE-
CIAL CONCERN, State
of Idaho, Category B
**DO NOT COLLECT:
PROTECTED SPECIES**

This phase is most commonly encountered near the Colorado
River in Arizona and California.

DATE:

LOCATION:

HABITAT:

WEATHER:

SIZE/SEX:

REMARKS:

**Ground Snake
(banded phase)**
Sonora semiannulata

STATUS: SPECIES OF SPE-
CIAL CONCERN, State
of Idaho, Category B
**DO NOT COLLECT:
PROTECTED SPECIES**

DATE:

LOCATION:

HABITAT:

WEATHER:

SIZE/SEX:

REMARKS:

**Ground Snake
(collared phase)**
Sonora semiannulata

STATUS: SPECIES OF SPE-
CIAL CONCERN, State
of Idaho, Category B
**DO NOT COLLECT:
PROTECTED SPECIES**

DATE:

LOCATION:

HABITAT:

WEATHER:

SIZE/SEX:

REMARKS:

DATE:

LOCATION:

HABITAT:

WEATHER:

SIZE/SEX:

REMARKS:

Additional species, subspecies, and forms

COMMON NAME:

SCIENTIFIC NAME:

DATE:

LOCATION:

HABITAT:

WEATHER:

SIZE/SEX:

REMARKS:

COMMON NAME:

SCIENTIFIC NAME:

DATE:

LOCATION:

HABITAT:

WEATHER:

SIZE/SEX:

REMARKS:

COMMON NAME:

SCIENTIFIC NAME:

MUD AND RAINBOW SNAKES

Family: Colubridae
Genus: *Farancia*

THESE TWO species are beautiful, large, very aquatic, seldom-seen snakes that inhabit the southeastern United States. Both species feed on large aquatic salamanders—including sirens and amphiumas—and true eels. Although the mud snake is often considerably larger, both species may exceed 5 feet in length. The rainbow snake, originally described as a member of the genus *Abastor*, is one of the most beautiful snakes found in the United States. Both mud snakes and rainbow snakes frequent spring-fed riparian habitats. Eastern and Western Mud snakes occasionally intergrade in extreme western Florida, southeastern Alabama, and parts of western Georgia.

Western Mud Snake

Farancia abacura reinwardti

STATUS: SPECIES OF SPE-CIAL CONCERN, states of Oklahoma and Kentucky
WATCHLIST SPECIES, DECLINING, State of Missouri
DO NOT COLLECT: PROTECTED SPECIES

DATE:

LOCATION:

HABITAT:

WEATHER:

SIZE/SEX:

REMARKS:

DATE:

LOCATION:

HABITAT:

WEATHER:

SIZE/SEX:

REMARKS:

Eastern Mud Snake
Farancia abacura abacura

DATE:

LOCATION:

HABITAT:

WEATHER:

SIZE/SEX:

REMARKS:

Rainbow Snake
Farancia erytrogramma erytrogramma

STATUS: ENDANGERED, states of Mississippi and Louisiana (considered imperiled in Louisiana and vulnerable to extirpation.) ENDANGERED OR EXTIRPATED, State of Maryland
DO NOT COLLECT: PROTECTED SPECIES

DATE:

LOCATION:

HABITAT:

WEATHER:

SIZE/SEX:

REMARKS:

South Florida Rainbow Snake
Farancia erytrogramma seminola

**Additional species,
subspecies, and forms**

COMMON NAME:

SCIENTIFIC NAME:

DATE:

LOCATION:

HABITAT:

WEATHER:

SIZE/SEX:

REMARKS:

COMMON NAME:

SCIENTIFIC NAME:

DATE:

LOCATION:

HABITAT:

WEATHER:

SIZE/SEX:

REMARKS:

COMMON NAME:

SCIENTIFIC NAME:

DATE:

LOCATION:

HABITAT:

WEATHER:

SIZE/SEX:

REMARKS:

GREEN SNAKES

Family: Colubridae
Genus: *Opheodrys*

THIS GENUS is represented in the United States by two species: the Smooth Green Snake and the Rough Green Snake. The Smooth Green Snake is a small, smooth-scaled terrestrial form that attains a maximum length of 24 inches. It is found in the northeastern and midwestern United States, and isolated disjunct populations exist in western mountains. The Rough Green Snake is a longer, more slender form which is lighter in coloration and more arboreal. The Rough Green Snake is found in the southeastern and south central United States. Both species are harmless and feed mostly on insects and arachnids. Both species are oviparous.

DATE:

LOCATION:

HABITAT:

WEATHER:

SIZE/SEX:

REMARKS:

Eastern Smooth Green Snake
Opheodrys vernalis vernalis

STATUS: SPECIES OF SPECIAL CONCERN, State of North Carolina
DO NOT COLLECT: PROTECTED SPECIES

Western Smooth Green Snake

Opheodrys vernalis blanchardi

STATUS: ENDANGERED, states of Texas and Missouri
THREATENED, states of Indiana and Iowa
SPECIES OF SPECIAL CONCERN, State of Idaho, Category C
DO NOT COLLECT: PROTECTED SPECIES

DATE:

LOCATION:

HABITAT:

WEATHER:

SIZE/SEX:

REMARKS:

Western Smooth Green Snake (tan phase)

Opheodrys vernalis blanchardi

STATUS: ENDANGERED, states of Texas and Missouri
THREATENED, states of Indiana and Iowa
SPECIES OF SPECIAL CONCERN, State of Idaho, Category C
DO NOT COLLECT: PROTECTED SPECIES

This rather pale color phase is commonly encountered in the upper Midwest.

DATE:

LOCATION:

HABITAT:

WEATHER:

SIZE/SEX:

REMARKS:

Rough Green Snake

Opheodrys aestivus

STATUS: THREATENED, State of Pennsylvania
SPECIES OF SPECIAL CONCERN, State of Indiana
DO NOT COLLECT: PROTECTED SPECIES

DATE:

LOCATION:

HABITAT:

WEATHER:

SIZE/SEX:

REMARKS:

DATE: **Additional species,
                                                subspecies, and forms**
LOCATION:
                                                COMMON NAME:
HABITAT:

WEATHER:
                                                SCIENTIFIC NAME:
SIZE/SEX:

REMARKS

DATE: COMMON NAME:

LOCATION:

HABITAT: SCIENTIFIC NAME:

WEATHER:

SIZE/SEX:

REMARKS

DATE: COMMON NAME:

LOCATION:

HABITAT: SCIENTIFIC NAME:

WEATHER:

SIZE/SEX:

REMARKS

RACERS, WHIPSNAKES, COACHWHIPS, AND PATCHNOSE SNAKES

Family: Colubridae
Genera: *Coluber, Masticophis,* and *Salvadora*

THESE ARE our fastest moving snakes. Snakes from these genera are quite slender and all are diurnal. Often the only part of this snake that can be seen is the tip of its tail as it rapidly disappears in the brush. Racers (*Coluber*) and whipsnakes (*Masticophis*) are closely related; both have slender necks and large eyes. Patchnose snakes (*Salvadora*) have an enlarged rostral scale which curls back over the snout. These snakes are usually smaller than racers, coachwhips, or whipsnakes; adults range from 22 to more than 40 inches. Adult racers range in length from 20 to 40 inches for the Mexican Racer (*Coluber constrictor oaxaca*), to slightly over 6 feet for the Northern Black Racer (*Coluber constrictor constrictor*). Coachwhips and whipsnakes occasionally reach greater lengths: the record for an Eastern Coachwhip (*Masticophis flagellum flagellum*) is 8 feet 4 inches. Racers and whipsnakes are highly excitable and often bite when first handled.

Young racers and coachwhips tend to be strongly patterned until their second or third summer, when they attain their adult coloration. Adult coachwhips vary dramatically in color. Some adults of a subspecies may be bright salmon-pink in color, while others of the same subspecies are jet black, and still others may be a drab brown. Young whipsnakes and patchnose snakes are generally patterned like adults.

Whipsnakes, coachwhips, and patchnose snakes feed mainly on lizards and snakes and occasionally take small rodents and birds. Racers feed mainly on rodents and birds but also take lizards, snakes, and amphibians on occasion. It should be noted that racers, despite the name *Coluber constrictor*, are not constrictors. Snakes of these genera are all oviparous.

DATE:

LOCATION:

HABITAT:

WEATHER:

SIZE/SEX:

REMARKS:

Northern Black Racer
Coluber constrictor constrictor

STATUS: ENDANGERED,
State of Maine
WATCHLIST SPECIES,
State of New York
**DO NOT COLLECT:
PROTECTED SPECIES**

DATE:

LOCATION:

HABITAT:

WEATHER:

SIZE/SEX:

REMARKS:

Southern Black Racer
Coluber constrictor priapus

DATE:

LOCATION:

HABITAT:

WEATHER:

SIZE/SEX:

REMARKS:

Brownchin Racer
Coluber constrictor helvigularis

Blue Racer
Coluber constrictor foxii
STATUS: SPECIES OF SPE-
CIAL CONCERN, State
of Minnesota
**DO NOT COLLECT:
PROTECTED SPECIES**

DATE:

LOCATION:

HABITAT:

WEATHER:

SIZE/SEX:

REMARKS:

Everglades Racer
*Coluber constrictor
paludicola*

DATE:

LOCATION:

HABITAT:

WEATHER:

SIZE/SEX:

REMARKS:

Eastern Yellowbelly Racer
*Coluber constrictor
flaviventris*

Color may be somewhat variable throughout range.

DATE:

LOCATION:

HABITAT:

WEATHER:

SIZE/SEX:

REMARKS:

DATE:

LOCATION:

HABITAT:

WEATHER:

SIZE/SEX:

REMARKS:

Blackmask Racer
Coluber constrictor latrunculus

Color may be somewhat variable throughout range.

DATE:

LOCATION:

HABITAT:

WEATHER:

SIZE/SEX:

REMARKS:

Western Yellowbelly Racer
Coluber constrictor mormon

Pattern and/or color may be somewhat variable.

DATE:

LOCATION:

HABITAT:

WEATHER:

SIZE/SEX:

REMARKS:

Buttermilk Racer
Coluber constrictor anthicus

Tan Racer
*Coluber constrictor
etheridgei*

DATE:

LOCATION:

HABITAT:

WEATHER:

SIZE/SEX:

REMARKS:

Mexican Racer
Coluber constrictor oaxaca

DATE:

LOCATION:

HABITAT:

WEATHER:

SIZE/SEX:

REMARKS:

Eastern Coachwhip Snake
*Masticophis flagellum
flagellum*

STATUS: THREATENED,
State of Illinois
EXTIRPATED OR EX-
TINCT, State of
Kentucky
**DO NOT COLLECT:
PROTECTED SPECIES**

Pattern and/or color may be extremely variable throughout range.

DATE:

LOCATION:

HABITAT:

WEATHER:

SIZE/SEX:

REMARKS:

The black phase with reddish coloration on the tail is found in portions of Arkansas, Oklahoma, Kansas, and Missouri.

DATE:

LOCATION:

HABITAT:

WEATHER:

SIZE/SEX:

REMARKS:

Eastern Coachwhip Snake (black phase)
Masticophis flagellum flagellum

Individuals from southern Georgia and northern Florida are usually very pale in color with little dark coloration.

DATE:

LOCATION:

HABITAT:

WEATHER:

SIZE/SEX:

REMARKS:

Eastern Coachwhip Snake (pale phase)
Masticophis flagellum flagellum

DATE:

LOCATION:

HABITAT:

WEATHER:

SIZE/SEX:

REMARKS:

Red Coachwhip Snake
Masticophis flagellum piceus

Western Black Coachwhip Snake (black phase of Red Coachwhip)
Masticophis flagellum piceus

This dark morph, often completely black, is quite common in some areas of southern Arizona, particularly near Tucson and Phoenix. Some individuals are mixed red and black.

DATE:

LOCATION:

HABITAT:

WEATHER:

SIZE/SEX:

REMARKS:

Lined Coachwhip Snake
Masticophis flagellum lineatulus

DATE:

LOCATION:

HABITAT:

WEATHER:

SIZE/SEX:

REMARKS:

Central Coachwhip Snake
Masticophis flagellum testaceus

DATE:

LOCATION:

HABITAT:

WEATHER:

SIZE/SEX:

REMARKS:

DATE:

LOCATION:

HABITAT:

WEATHER:

SIZE/SEX:

REMARKS:

Central Coachwhip Snake (red phase)
Masticophis flagellum testaceus

DATE:

LOCATION:

HABITAT:

WEATHER:

SIZE/SEX:

REMARKS:

San Joaquin Coachwhip Snake
Masticophis flagellum ruddocki

Pattern and/or color may be somewhat variable throughout range.

DATE:

LOCATION:

HABITAT:

WEATHER:

SIZE/SEX:

REMARKS:

Sonoran Coachwhip Snake
Masticophis flagellum cingulum

**Baja California
Coachwhip (light phase)**
*Masticophis flagellum
fulginosus*

DATE:

LOCATION:

HABITAT:

WEATHER:

SIZE/SEX:

REMARKS:

**Baja California
Coachwhip (dark phase)**
*Masticophis flagellum
fulginosus*

DATE:

LOCATION:

HABITAT:

WEATHER:

SIZE/SEX:

REMARKS:

Chaparral Whipsnake
*Masticophis lateralis
lateralis*

This is a subspecies of California Whipsnake.

DATE:

LOCATION:

HABITAT:

WEATHER:

SIZE/SEX:

REMARKS:

This is a subspecies of California Whipsnake.

DATE:

LOCATION:

HABITAT:

WEATHER:

SIZE/SEX:

REMARKS:

Alameda Whipsnake
Masticophis lateralis euryxanthus

STATUS: THREATENED, State of California Candidate, Federal endangered or threatened species listing
DO NOT COLLECT: PROTECTED SPECIES

DATE:

LOCATION:

HABITAT:

WEATHER:

SIZE/SEX:

REMARKS:

Central Texas Whipsnake
Masticophis taeniatus girardi

DATE:

LOCATION:

HABITAT:

WEATHER:

SIZE/SEX:

REMARKS:

Desert Striped Whipsnake
Masticophis taeniatus taeniatus

Schott's Whipsnake
Masticophis taeniatus schotti

DATE:

LOCATION:

HABITAT:

WEATHER:

SIZE/SEX:

REMARKS:

Ruthven's Whipsnake
Masticophis taeniatus ruthveni

DATE:

LOCATION:

HABITAT:

WEATHER:

SIZE/SEX:

REMARKS:

Sonoran Whipsnake
Masticophis bilineatus bilineatus

DATE:

LOCATION:

HABITAT:

WEATHER:

SIZE/SEX:

REMARKS:

It should be noted that most, if not all, of the range of this subspecies is located within the boundaries of Organ Pipe Cactus National Monument, where collection of wildlife is prohibited.

Ajo Mountain Whipsnake
Masticophis bilineatus lineolatus

DATE:

LOCATION:

HABITAT:

WEATHER:

SIZE/SEX:

REMARKS:

DATE:

LOCATION:

HABITAT:

WEATHER:

SIZE/SEX:

REMARKS:

Plateau Patchnose Snake, Mountain Patchnose Snake
Salvadora grahamiae grahamiae

DATE:

LOCATION:

HABITAT:

WEATHER:

SIZE/SEX:

REMARKS:

Texas Patchnose Snake
Salvadora grahamiae lineata

Desert Patchnose Snake
*Salvadora hexalepis
hexalepis*

DATE:

LOCATION:

HABITAT:

WEATHER:

SIZE/SEX:

REMARKS:

Mojave Patchnose Snake
*Salvadora hexalepis
mojavensis*

STATUS: CANDIDATE,
endangered or threatened
species listing, State of
Utah

DATE:

LOCATION:

HABITAT:

WEATHER:

SIZE/SEX:

REMARKS:

Coast Patchnose Snake
*Salvadora hexalepis
virgultea*

STATUS: CANDIDATE,
Federal endangered or
threatened species listing

DATE:

LOCATION:

HABITAT:

WEATHER:

SIZE/SEX:

REMARKS:

Some herpetologists regard this form as a distinct and separate species, and not a member of the *hexalepis* group.

DATE:

LOCATION:

HABITAT:

WEATHER:

SIZE/SEX:

REMARKS:

Big Bend Patchnose Snake
Salvadora hexalepis deserticola

DATE:

LOCATION:

HABITAT:

WEATHER:

SIZE/SEX:

REMARKS:

Additional species, subspecies, and forms

COMMON NAME:

SCIENTIFIC NAME:

DATE:

LOCATION:

HABITAT:

WEATHER:

SIZE/SEX:

REMARKS:

COMMON NAME:

SCIENTIFIC NAME:

SPECKLED RACERS AND INDIGO SNAKES

Family: Colubridae
Genera: *Drymobius* and *Drymarchon*

THE RANGES of both indigo snakes and speckled racers extend southward from the southern United States through Mexico and Central America to South America. The genus *Drymarchon* includes the Eastern Indigo Snake, which is the largest snake native to the United States and may exceed 8½ feet in length. The indigo is surprisingly fast for its size. Like kingsnakes, indigo snakes often eat other snakes, including rattlers, and are believed to be partially immune to pit-viper venom. This beautiful species is now considered threatened and has become rare in many parts of its range due to habitat destruction and overcollecting. Collecting or possession of indigo snakes is prohibited by law.

The Texas Indigo Snake is also a very large snake, occasionally reaching 8 feet. The Speckled Racer is much smaller, reaching 3 to 4 feet in length. As its name would imply, the Speckled Racer is quite agile. This species is very common south of the border and occasionally strays north of the Rio Grande into the Brownsville area of extreme southeastern Texas.

DATE:

LOCATION:

HABITAT:

WEATHER:

SIZE/SEX:

REMARKS:

Eastern Indigo Snake
Drymarchon corais couperi

STATUS: ENDANGERED, State of Mississippi THREATENED, Federal, states of Georgia, Florida, and Alabama
DO NOT COLLECT: PROTECTED SPECIES

DATE:

LOCATION:

HABITAT:

WEATHER:

SIZE/SEX:

REMARKS:

Texas Indigo Snake
Drymarchon corais erebennus

STATUS: THREATENED, State of Texas
DO NOT COLLECT: PROTECTED SPECIES

DATE:

LOCATION:

HABITAT:

WEATHER:

SIZE/SEX:

REMARKS:

Speckled Racer
Drymobius margaritiferus margaritiferus

STATUS: ENDANGERED, State of Texas
DO NOT COLLECT: PROTECTED SPECIES

Additional species, subspecies, and forms

COMMON NAME:

SCIENTIFIC NAME:

DATE:

LOCATION:

HABITAT:

WEATHER:

SIZE/SEX:

REMARKS:

COMMON NAME:

SCIENTIFIC NAME:

DATE:

LOCATION:

HABITAT:

WEATHER:

SIZE/SEX:

REMARKS:

COMMON NAME:

SCIENTIFIC NAME:

DATE:

LOCATION:

HABITAT:

WEATHER:

SIZE/SEX:

REMARKS:

PINE, BULL, GOPHER, AND GLOSSY SNAKES

Family: Colubridae
Genera: *Pituophis* and *Arizona*

SPECIES OF the genus *Pituophis* are usually called pine snakes in the East and the South, bull snakes in the Midwest, and gopher snakes in the West. Some forms are among the largest of American snakes, occasionally exceeding 7 or 8 feet in length. These snakes are powerful constrictors that feed mainly on rodents and are usually valued by farmers and ranchers. Most species will hiss loudly and rattle their tails rapidly when first approached. In the eastern and southeastern United States, pine snakes are usually considered uncommon to rare and are very secretive in habits. In many regions of the western United States, however, gopher or bull snakes are often the most abundant species. Pine, bull, and gopher snakes are generally diurnal or crepuscular. Unfortunately, they are often killed on sight because of their resemblance to rattlesnakes.

Glossy snakes (*Arizona*) are related to the gopher and bull snakes but, unlike the gopher snakes, these forms are strictly nocturnal. More secretive in habits, they are less frequently observed. The glossy snake resembles a faded bull or gopher snake. Maximum length is approximately 5 feet, but individuals are usually under 3 feet. Like the bull and gopher snakes, glossy snakes are constrictors and feed on rodents, lizards, and other snakes. Snakes from both genera are egg-layers.

Northern Pine Snake
*Pituophis melanoleucus
melanoleucus*

STATUS: ENDANGERED
or EXTIRPATED, State of
Maryland (not verified
within the past 15 years);
THREATENED, states of
Tennessee, Kentucky, and
New Jersey; SPECIES OF
SPECIAL CONCERN,
State of North Carolina;
CANDIDATE, Federal en-
dangered or threatened
species listing; **DO NOT
COLLECT: PROTECTED
SPECIES**

DATE:

LOCATION:

HABITAT:

WEATHER:

SIZE/SEX:

REMARKS:

Florida Pine Snake
*Pituophis melanoleucus
mugitus*

STATUS: SPECIES OF
SPECIAL CONCERN,
State of Florida
CANDIDATE, Federal en-
dangered or threatened
species listing
**DO NOT COLLECT:
PROTECTED SPECIES**

DATE:

LOCATION:

HABITAT:

WEATHER:

SIZE/SEX:

REMARKS:

Florida Pine Snake
(patternless phase)
*Pituophis melanoleucus
mugitus*

This beautiful morph is known from several localities in Central
Florida. Like the patterned phase of the Florida Pine Snake, this
snake cannot be bought, sold, or possessed for sale in the State of
Florida.

DATE:

LOCATION:

HABITAT:

WEATHER:

SIZE/SEX:

REMARKS:

DATE:

LOCATION:

HABITAT:

WEATHER:

SIZE/SEX:

REMARKS:

Black Pine Snake
*Pituophis melanoleucus
lodingi*

STATUS: ENDANGERED,
states of Mississippi and
Louisiana (Considered
critically imperiled in
Louisiana—especially
vulnerable to extirpation.)
CANDIDATE, Federal en-
dangered or threatened
species listing
**DO NOT COLLECT:
PROTECTED SPECIES**

DATE:

LOCATION:

HABITAT:

WEATHER:

SIZE/SEX:

REMARKS:

Louisiana Pine Snake
*Pituophis melanoleucus
ruthveni*

STATUS: ENDANGERED,
State of Texas
CANDIDATE, Federal en-
dangered or threatened
species listing
RARE AND LOCAL,
State of Louisiana, where
it is considered vulner-
able to extirpation
**DO NOT COLLECT:
PROTECTED SPECIES**

Although very rare, several nearly pure black, or melanistic, individuals have been encountered in eastern Texas.

DATE:

LOCATION:

HABITAT:

WEATHER:

SIZE/SEX:

REMARKS:

**Louisiana Pine Snake
(black phase)**
*Pituophis melanoleucus
ruthveni*

STATUS: ENDANGERED,
State of Texas
CANDIDATE, Federal en-
dangered or threatened
species listing
**DO NOT COLLECT:
PROTECTED SPECIES**

Bull Snake
Pituophis melanoleucus sayi

The pattern is somewhat variable with this subspecies, usually darker in the eastern part of its range.

STATUS: SPECIES OF SPE-
CIAL CONCERN, State
of Minnesota
**DO NOT COLLECT:
PROTECTED SPECIES**

DATE:

LOCATION:

HABITAT:

WEATHER:

SIZE/SEX:

REMARKS:

Sonoran Gopher Snake
*Pituophis melanoleucus
affinis*

DATE:

LOCATION:

HABITAT:

WEATHER:

SIZE/SEX:

REMARKS:

**Great Basin Gopher
Snake**
*Pituophis melanoleucus
deserticola*

DATE:

LOCATION:

HABITAT:

WEATHER:

SIZE/SEX:

REMARKS:

DATE:

LOCATION:

HABITAT:

WEATHER:

SIZE/SEX:

REMARKS:

Pacific Gopher Snake
Pituophis melanoleucus catenifer

DATE:

LOCATION:

HABITAT:

WEATHER:

SIZE/SEX:

REMARKS:

San Diego Gopher Snake
Pituophis melanoleucus annectens

DATE:

LOCATION:

HABITAT:

WEATHER:

SIZE/SEX:

REMARKS:

Santa Cruz Gopher Snake
Pituophis melanoleucus pumilis

STATUS: CANDIDATE, Federal endangered or threatened species listing

Texas Glossy Snake
Arizona elegans arenicola

DATE:

LOCATION:

HABITAT:

WEATHER:

SIZE/SEX:

REMARKS:

Kansas Glossy Snake
Arizona elegans elegans

DATE:

LOCATION:

HABITAT:

WEATHER:

SIZE/SEX:

REMARKS:

Painted Desert Glossy Snake
Arizona elegans philipi

DATE:

LOCATION:

HABITAT:

WEATHER:

SIZE/SEX:

REMARKS:

DATE:

LOCATION:

HABITAT:

WEATHER:

SIZE/SEX:

REMARKS:

Arizona Glossy Snake
Arizona elegans noctivaga

DATE:

LOCATION:

HABITAT:

WEATHER:

SIZE/SEX:

REMARKS:

California Glossy Snake
Arizona elegans occidentalis

DATE:

LOCATION:

HABITAT:

WEATHER:

SIZE/SEX:

REMARKS:

Desert Glossy Snake
Arizona elegans eburnata

STATUS: CANDIDATE, endangered or threatened species listing, State of Utah

Mojave Glossy Snake
Arizona elegans candida

DATE:

LOCATION:

HABITAT:

WEATHER:

SIZE/SEX:

REMARKS:

**Additional species,
subspecies, and forms**

COMMON NAME:

SCIENTIFIC NAME:

DATE:

LOCATION:

HABITAT:

WEATHER:

SIZE/SEX:

REMARKS:

COMMON NAME:

SCIENTIFIC NAME:

DATE:

LOCATION:

HABITAT:

WEATHER:

SIZE/SEX:

REMARKS:

RAT SNAKES

Family: Colubridae
Genera: *Elaphe, Bogertophis,* and *Senticolis*

RAT SNAKES are among our largest and most beautiful species. This widespread group comprises several subgroups. In the United States, rat snakes are represented by three genera: *Elaphe, Bogertophis,* and *Senticolis.* Until fairly recently, *Elaphe* was the only recognized genus of rat snakes, comprising both *Bogertophis* and *Senticolis.*

The genus *Elaphe* comprises four subgroups. The *obsoleta* group, which includes the largest, most widespread and abundant forms, is represented by five subspecies and several more-or-less distinct color phases. The *guttata* group, commonly called corn snakes, is represented by two subspecies. The *vulpina* group, or fox snakes, includes two known subspecies, and the *"bairdi"* group includes only one subspecies in this country.

Subspecies of *Elaphe obsoleta* vary considerably in pattern and color, adults ranging in color from nearly solid black to bright yellow and orange and in pattern from striped to plain or blotched. Juveniles of all subspecies are usually grayish and blotched. Large black rat snakes may, on very rare occasions, exceed 8 feet in length.

Members of the *guttata* group, or corn snakes, are generally smaller than the *obsoleta* species, the former attaining a maximum length of 6 feet. These snakes, especially the corn snakes and rosy rat snakes, are the most attractive of this genus. Fox snakes (*vulpina*), medium to large, blotched snakes exceeding 5 feet in length, are found in several midwestern states.

Both the Baird's Rat Snake (*Elaphe bairdi*) and the Western Green Rat Snake (*Senticolis triaspis intermedia*) are restricted to the southwestern United States. The Western Green Rat Snake barely enters the U.S. in several mountain ranges in extreme southeastern Arizona and southwestern New Mexico, while the Baird's Rat Snake is found in several mountain ranges of the Chihuahuan Desert in West Texas. Both species average 3 to 4 feet in length. Some authorities group the Baird's Rat Snake with the *obsoleta* group.

The genera *Bogertophis* and *Senticolis* have a limited distribution north of the Mexican border. *Bogertophis* is represented by only two species in the United States and *Senticolis* by only one. The Trans-Pecos Rat Snake (*Bogertophis subocularis subocularis*) is a resident of the Chihuahuan Desert which averages 3 to 4 feet.

All rat snakes are powerful constrictors that prey mainly on rodents and birds.

Corn Snake, Red Rat Snake
Elaphe guttata guttata

STATUS: ENDANGERED, State of New Jersey
SPECIES OF SPECIAL CONCERN, State of Kentucky
DO NOT COLLECT: PROTECTED SPECIES

DATE:

LOCATION:

HABITAT:

WEATHER:

SIZE/SEX:

REMARKS:

Corn Snake (striped phase)
Elaphe guttata guttata

Corn Snakes with well-defined longitudinal stripes are occasionally encountered in the area of Vero Beach, Indian River County, Florida. These stripes generally become more conspicuous when the snake is in shed.

DATE:

LOCATION:

HABITAT:

WEATHER:

SIZE/SEX:

REMARKS:

This phase, which lacks the red coloration of the typical phase, is frequently encountered in Glades, Hendry, Lee, and Collier counties in southwestern Florida and may closely resemble *Elaphe guttata emoryi*.

Corn Snake (anerythristic phase)
Elaphe guttata guttata

DATE:

LOCATION:

HABITAT:

WEATHER:

SIZE/SEX:

REMARKS:

This is no longer considered a distinct subspecies but is now believed by many to be a color form of *Elaphe guttata guttata*.

Rosy Rat Snake
Elaphe guttata rosacea

STATUS: SPECIES OF SPECIAL CONCERN, State of Florida
DO NOT COLLECT: PROTECTED SPECIES

DATE:

LOCATION:

HABITAT:

WEATHER:

SIZE/SEX:

REMARKS:

DATE:

LOCATION:

HABITAT:

WEATHER:

SIZE/SEX:

REMARKS:

Great Plains Rat Snake
Elaphe guttata emoryi

STATUS: THREATENED, State of Illinois
DO NOT COLLECT: PROTECTED SPECIES

Western Fox Snake
Elaphe vulpina vulpina

STATUS: ENDANGERED,
State of Missouri
SPECIES OF SPECIAL
CONCERN, State of
Minnesota
**DO NOT COLLECT:
PROTECTED SPECIES**

DATE:

LOCATION:

HABITAT:

WEATHER:

SIZE/SEX:

REMARKS:

Eastern Fox Snake
Elaphe vulpina gloydi

STATUS: THREATENED,
State of Michigan
**DO NOT COLLECT:
PROTECTED SPECIES**

DATE:

LOCATION:

HABITAT:

WEATHER:

SIZE/SEX:

REMARKS:

Black Rat Snake
Elaphe obsoleta obsoleta

STATUS: ENDANGERED,
State of Massachusetts
SPECIES OF SPECIAL
CONCERN, State of
Minnesota
Considered IMPERILED
in Wisconsin and vulner-
able to extirpation from
state
WATCHLIST SPECIES,
State of New York
**DO NOT COLLECT:
PROTECTED SPECIES**

DATE:

LOCATION:

HABITAT:

WEATHER:

SIZE/SEX:

REMARKS:

DATE:

LOCATION:

HABITAT:

WEATHER:

SIZE/SEX:

REMARKS:

Yellow Rat Snake
Elaphe obsoleta quadrivittata

This color phase of the Yellow Rat Snake retains much of its juvenile pattern as an adult, often having both stripes and blotches. This morph is no longer recognized as a distinct subspecies. It is native to the Florida Keys.

Key Rat Snake, Deckert's Rat Snake
Elaphe obsoleta deckerti

DATE:

LOCATION:

HABITAT:

WEATHER:

SIZE/SEX:

REMARKS:

This intergrade is included in the main text because it is the commonly encountered *obsoleta* form in a long stretch of piedmont and coastal plain from North Carolina south to Georgia, where neither the Black Rat Snake nor the Yellow Rat Snake can be found in pure form.

Greenish Rat Snake
Elaphe o. obsoleta / o. quadrivittata intergrade

DATE:

LOCATION:

HABITAT:

WEATHER:

SIZE/SEX:

REMARKS:

Everglades Rat Snake
Elaphe obsoleta rossalleni

This species is declining in pure form.

DATE:

LOCATION:

HABITAT:

WEATHER:

SIZE/SEX:

REMARKS:

**Gulf Hammock Rat
Snake**

Elaphe obsoleta williamsi

This is no longer recognized as a distinct subspecies but is considered an intergrade between the Gray Rat Snake (*Elaphe obsoleta spiloides*) and the Yellow Rat Snake (*Elaphe obsoleta quadrivittata*) by many herpetologists. This intergrade is included in the main part of the text because it is the only form of *obsoleta* that occurs in the Gulf Hammock region (an area roughly 20 by 95 miles in size) of northwestern Florida. Adults are patterned with both stripes and saddles.

DATE:

LOCATION:

HABITAT:

WEATHER:

SIZE/SEX:

REMARKS:

Gray Rat Snake
Elaphe obsoleta spiloides

DATE:

LOCATION:

HABITAT:

WEATHER:

SIZE/SEX:

REMARKS:

DATE:

LOCATION:

HABITAT:

WEATHER:

SIZE/SEX:

REMARKS:

Texas Rat Snake
Elaphe obsoleta lindheimeri

DATE:

LOCATION:

HABITAT:

WEATHER:

SIZE/SEX:

REMARKS:

Baird's Rat Snake
Elaphe bairdi

DATE:

LOCATION:

HABITAT:

WEATHER:

SIZE/SEX:

REMARKS:

Western Green Rat Snake
*Senticolis triaspis
intermedia*

STATUS: ENDANGERED,
State of New Mexico,
Group 2
**DO NOT COLLECT:
PROTECTED SPECIES**

Baja California Rat Snake
Bogertophis rosaliae

An isolated population of this Mexican species has been discovered near the Mexican border in Imperial County, California.

DATE:

LOCATION:

HABITAT:

WEATHER:

SIZE/SEX:

REMARKS:

Trans-Pecos Rat Snake
Bogertophis subocularis subocularis

DATE:

LOCATION:

HABITAT:

WEATHER:

SIZE/SEX:

REMARKS:

Trans-Pecos Rat Snake (blond phase)
Bogertophis subocularis subocularis

This beautiful morph is a very light phase that lacks the longitudinal stripes found on the typical form. It is generally restricted to the Terlingua Creek drainage in Brewster County, Texas. In the author's opinion, the "blond suboc," as it is called, is among the most beautiful snakes native to the United States.

DATE:

LOCATION:

HABITAT:

WEATHER:

SIZE/SEX:

REMARKS:

Individuals from the Franklin Mountains area of northwestern Texas differ from the typical Trans-Pecos Rat Snake in that they usually have a steel-gray ground color.

Trans-Pecos Rat Snake (gray phase)
Bogertophis subocularis subocularis

DATE:

LOCATION:

HABITAT:

WEATHER:

SIZE/SEX:

REMARKS:

DATE:

LOCATION:

HABITAT:

WEATHER:

SIZE/SEX:

REMARKS:

Additional species, subspecies, and forms

COMMON NAME:

SCIENTIFIC NAME:

DATE:

LOCATION:

HABITAT:

WEATHER:

SIZE/SEX:

REMARKS:

COMMON NAME:

SCIENTIFIC NAME:

KINGSNAKES AND MILK SNAKES

Family: Colubridae
Genus: *Lampropeltis*

THE GENUS *Lampropeltis* comprises the kingsnakes and milk snakes, which are strictly New World serpents ranging from southern Canada south through much of the United States, Mexico, and Central America to northern South America. Kingsnakes are generally larger than milk snakes; several kingsnake subspecies exceed 6 feet in length, while the length of an adult milk snake is usually less than 3 feet. Kingsnakes are usually black or brown with white or yellow markings. Milk snakes are usually tricolored with either rings or blotches. Kingsnakes of the species *getulus* are often highly variable in color and pattern.

Both kingsnakes and milk snakes are ophiophages (snake eaters), generally immune to the venom of native pit vipers, but also feed on rodents and birds. Kingsnakes and milk snakes occupy a variety of habitats from humid southern pine woods to high mountain forests to arid southwestern deserts. All species of kingsnakes and milk snakes are oviparous, and all are powerful constrictors. Many forms of the tricolored milk snakes are often mistaken for the venomous coral snakes. Several of the tricolored snakes are highly prized by reptile collectors, who have depleted many populations. Virtually every subspecies of milk snake and kingsnake has now been successfully bred in captivity. Anyone considering keeping one of these snakes in captivity should obtain it from a captive breeding program.

Pattern and/or color may be somewhat variable throughout range.

DATE:

LOCATION:

HABITAT:

WEATHER:

SIZE/SEX:

REMARKS:

Eastern Kingsnake
Lampropeltis getulus getulus

Many individuals from the southern part of its range, particularly Georgia and South Carolina, have a rich, chocolate brown ground color rather than the black of the typical form.

DATE:

LOCATION:

HABITAT:

WEATHER:

SIZE/SEX:

REMARKS:

Eastern Kingsnake (chocolate phase)
Lampropeltis getulus getulus

DATE:

LOCATION:

HABITAT:

WEATHER:

SIZE/SEX:

REMARKS:

Outer Banks Kingsnake
Lampropeltis getulus sticticeps

STATUS: SPECIES OF SPECIAL CONCERN, State of North Carolina
DO NOT COLLECT: PROTECTED SPECIES

South Florida Kingsnake, Brooks Kingsnake
Lampropeltis getulus brooksi

This beautiful golden-yellow morph is declining rapidly in the wild due to habitat destruction and overcollection. Occurrences of pure-form *brooksi* individuals are restricted to several isolated populations in extreme southern Florida. These are found amid populations of kingsnakes which look more like the typical "Peninsula" form.

DATE:

LOCATION:

HABITAT:

WEATHER:

SIZE/SEX:

REMARKS:

Florida Kingsnake (peninsula phase)
Lampropeltis getulus floridana

Pattern and/or color may be extremely variable throughout range.

DATE:

LOCATION:

HABITAT:

WEATHER:

SIZE/SEX:

REMARKS:

Blotched Kingsnake (Apalachicola phase of Florida Kingsnake)
Lampropeltis getulus goini

No longer considered a distinct subspecies, this form is now believed to be an intergrade between the Eastern and Florida kingsnakes. This morph is extremely variable in pattern and is generally restricted to the Apalachicola and Chipola riparian corridors in the Florida panhandle.

DATE:

LOCATION:

HABITAT:

WEATHER:

SIZE/SEX:

REMARKS:

DATE:

LOCATION:

HABITAT:

WEATHER:

SIZE/SEX:

REMARKS:

Speckled Kingsnake
Lampropeltis getulus holbrooki

STATUS: ENDANGERED, State of Iowa
DO NOT COLLECT: PROTECTED SPECIES

DATE:

LOCATION:

HABITAT:

WEATHER:

SIZE/SEX:

REMARKS:

Eastern Black Kingsnake
Lampropeltis getulus nigra

Pattern and/or color may be somewhat variable throughout range.

DATE:

LOCATION:

HABITAT:

WEATHER:

SIZE/SEX:

REMARKS:

Desert Kingsnake
Lampropeltis getulus splendida

**Desert Kingsnake
(chocolate phase)**
*Lampropeltis getulus
splendida*

Specimens with a rich, chocolate brown ground color are occasionally encountered in the Trans-Pecos region of Texas, as well as other areas.

DATE:

LOCATION:

HABITAT:

WEATHER:

SIZE/SEX:

REMARKS:

Mexican Black Kingsnake
*Lampropeltis getulus
nigritus*

DATE:

LOCATION:

HABITAT:

WEATHER:

SIZE/SEX:

REMARKS:

**California Kingsnake
(Yuma or desert phase)**
*Lampropeltis getulus
yumensis*

STATUS: CANDIDATE,
endangered or threatened
species listing, State of
Utah

This form occurs in the desert regions of Arizona and southern California. It often has highly contrasting bright black and white bands and some specimens look very much like the Eastern Kingsnake (*Lampropeltis getulus getulus*), although the white bands are usually wider in this morph. It is no longer recognized as a distinct subspecies.

DATE:

LOCATION:

HABITAT:

WEATHER:

SIZE/SEX:

REMARKS:

Pattern and/or color may be variable throughout range, usually black or dark brown with a series of white, yellow, or cream-colored crossbands. Captive breeding of this subspecies now produces a variety of color morphs, several of which cannot be found in the wild.

DATE:

LOCATION:

HABITAT:

WEATHER:

SIZE/SEX:

REMARKS:

California Kingsnake (banded phase)
Lampropeltis getulus californiae

STATUS: CANDIDATE, endangered or threatened species listing, State of Utah

---

Striped California Kings are not uncommon in southern California, especially in San Diego County, where this morph accounts for approximately one-third of the members of this species encountered in the field. This subspecies is the only striped subspecies of the *getulus* species. Occasionally specimens are found that have both longitudinal stripes and partial bands.

DATE:

LOCATION:

HABITAT:

WEATHER:

SIZE/SEX:

REMARKS:

California Kingsnake (striped phase)
Lampropeltis getulus californiae

STATUS: CANDIDATE, endangered or threatened species listing, State of Utah

---

In portions of the northern San Joaquin Valley of California, very dark specimens with very little pattern are sometimes encountered.

DATE:

LOCATION:

HABITAT:

WEATHER:

SIZE/SEX:

REMARKS:

California Kingsnake (melanistic phase)
Lampropeltis getulus californiae

**Sierra Mountain
Kingsnake**
*Lampropeltis zonata
multicincta*

DATE:

LOCATION:

HABITAT:

WEATHER:

SIZE/SEX:

REMARKS:

**Sierra Mountain
Kingsnake (black and
white phase)**
*Lampropeltis zonata
multicincta*

Individuals lacking red coloration are found occasionally in the central Sierra Nevadas, California.

DATE:

LOCATION:

HABITAT:

WEATHER:

SIZE/SEX:

REMARKS:

**Saint Helena Mountain
Kingsnake**
Lampropeltis zonata zonata

DATE:

LOCATION:

HABITAT:

WEATHER:

SIZE/SEX:

REMARKS:

DATE:

LOCATION:

HABITAT:

WEATHER:

SIZE/SEX:

REMARKS:

Coast Mountain Kingsnake
Lampropeltis zonata multifasciata

DATE:

LOCATION:

HABITAT:

WEATHER:

SIZE/SEX:

REMARKS:

San Bernardino Mountain Kingsnake
Lampropeltis zonata parvirubra

DATE:

LOCATION:

HABITAT:

WEATHER:

SIZE/SEX:

REMARKS:

San Diego Mountain Kingsnake
Lampropeltis zonata pulchra

STATUS: PROTECTED, State of California CANDIDATE, Federal endangered or threatened species listing
DO NOT COLLECT: PROTECTED SPECIES

**Arizona Mountain
Kingsnake**
*Lampropeltis pyromelana
pyromelana*

DATE:

LOCATION:

HABITAT:

WEATHER:

SIZE/SEX:

REMARKS:

**Utah Mountain
Kingsnake**
*Lampropeltis pyromelana
infralabialis*

STATUS: CANDIDATE,
endangered or threatened
species listing, State of
Utah

DATE:

LOCATION:

HABITAT:

WEATHER:

SIZE/SEX:

REMARKS:

**Huachuca Mountain
Kingsnake**
*Lampropeltis pyromelana
woodini*

This morph differs from the typical Arizona Mountain Kingsnake
in that it usually has fewer than 43 white bands. Many herpetologists disagree on whether this form should be recognized as a distinct subspecies. It is restricted in distribution to the Huachuca
Mountains of southern Arizona and adjacent ranges in Mexico.

DATE:

LOCATION:

HABITAT:

WEATHER:

SIZE/SEX:

REMARKS:

Pattern and/or color may be extremely variable throughout range.

DATE:

LOCATION:

HABITAT:

WEATHER:

SIZE/SEX:

REMARKS:

Mole Kingsnake, Brown Kingsnake
Lampropeltis calligaster rhombomaculata

DATE:

LOCATION:

HABITAT:

WEATHER:

SIZE/SEX:

REMARKS:

South Florida Mole Kingsnake
Lampropeltis calligaster occipitolineata

DATE:

LOCATION:

HABITAT:

WEATHER:

SIZE/SEX:

REMARKS:

Prairie Kingsnake
Lampropeltis calligaster calligaster

The Gray-banded Kingsnake may be North America's most variable snake, in pattern and color and with many geographically different morphs. Some *alterna* experts can tell specifically where a particular animal was found by the appearance of the snake. Four general morphs are found: the light Blair's phase, the dark Blair's phase, the light *alterna* phase and the dark *alterna* phase. The Blair's phase morphs are most commonly encountered in the eastern portion of the range, while the *alterna* phase morphs are more commonly found in the western portion. Gray-bands are immensely popular among reptile enthusiasts, and just about any variations imaginable are now available through captive breeding programs. The negative side of their popularity is the fact that collectors travel to West Texas every spring and summer from as far away as Europe and Australia to collect *alternas.* As a result, many wild populations of Gray-banded Kingsnakes have suffered significant declines.

Gray-banded Kingsnake (light Blair's phase)
Lampropeltis alterna

STATUS: CANDIDATE, protected status, State of New Mexico

DATE:

LOCATION:

HABITAT:

WEATHER:

SIZE/SEX:

REMARKS:

DATE:

LOCATION:

HABITAT:

WEATHER:

SIZE/SEX:

REMARKS:

**Gray-banded Kingsnake
(dark Blair's phase)**
Lampropeltis alterna

STATUS: CANDIDATE,
protected status, State of
New Mexico

DATE:

LOCATION:

HABITAT:

WEATHER:

SIZE/SEX:

REMARKS:

**Gray-banded Kingsnake
(light *alterna* phase)**
Lampropeltis alterna

STATUS: CANDIDATE,
protected status, State of
New Mexico

DATE:

LOCATION:

HABITAT:

WEATHER:

SIZE/SEX:

REMARKS:

**Gray-banded Kingsnake
(dark *alterna* phase)**
Lampropeltis alterna

STATUS: CANDIDATE,
protected status, State of
New Mexico

Scarlet Kingsnake

Lampropeltis triangulum elapsoides

STATUS: SPECIES OF SPE-
CIAL CONCERN, State
of Kentucky
**DO NOT COLLECT:
PROTECTED SPECIES**

DATE:

LOCATION:

HABITAT:

WEATHER:

SIZE/SEX:

REMARKS:

Eastern Milk Snake

Lampropeltis triangulum triangulum

STATUS: SPECIES OF SPE-
CIAL CONCERN, State
of Minnesota
**DO NOT COLLECT:
PROTECTED SPECIES**

Color may be extremely variable throughout range.

DATE:

LOCATION:

HABITAT:

WEATHER:

SIZE/SEX:

REMARKS:

Coastal Plain Milk Snake

Lampropeltis triangulum temporalis

This form is no longer recognized as a distinct subspecies by many authorities who consider it an intergrade between *Lampropeltis triangulum elapsoides* and *Lampropeltis triangulum triangulum*. This beautifully colored morph is the only milk snake found in much of the coastal plain of the Mid-Atlantic area from New Jersey south to North Carolina.

DATE:

LOCATION:

HABITAT:

WEATHER:

SIZE/SEX:

REMARKS:

DATE:

LOCATION:

HABITAT:

WEATHER:

SIZE/SEX:

REMARKS:

Louisiana Milk Snake
Lampropeltis triangulum amaura

STATUS: SPECIES OF SPE-
CIAL CONCERN, State
of Oklahoma
**DO NOT COLLECT:
PROTECTED SPECIES**

DATE:

LOCATION:

HABITAT:

WEATHER:

SIZE/SEX:

REMARKS:

Mexican Milk Snake
Lampropeltis triangulum annulata

In this handsome color phase, each of the crossbands, including the white or cream-colored bands, has an orange- or tangerine-colored tint.

DATE:

LOCATION:

HABITAT:

WEATHER:

SIZE/SEX:

REMARKS:

**Mexican Milk Snake
(tangerine phase)**
Lampropeltis triangulum annulata

New Mexico Milk Snake,
Big Bend Milk Snake
Lampropeltis triangulum
celaenops

Pattern and/or color may be somewhat variable.

DATE:

LOCATION:

HABITAT:

WEATHER:

SIZE/SEX:

REMARKS:

Central Plains Milk
Snake
Lampropeltis triangulum
gentilis

DATE:

LOCATION:

HABITAT:

WEATHER:

SIZE/SEX:

REMARKS:

Pale Milk Snake
Lampropeltis triangulum
multistrata

DATE:

LOCATION:

HABITAT:

WEATHER:

SIZE/SEX:

REMARKS:

DATE:

LOCATION:

HABITAT:

WEATHER:

SIZE/SEX:

REMARKS:

Red Milk Snake
Lampropeltis triangulum syspila

DATE:

LOCATION:

HABITAT:

WEATHER:

SIZE/SEX:

REMARKS:

Utah Milk Snake
Lampropeltis triangulum taylori

STATUS: CANDIDATE, endangered or threatened species listing, State of Utah

---

DATE:

LOCATION:

HABITAT:

WEATHER:

SIZE/SEX:

REMARKS:

Additional species, subspecies, and forms

COMMON NAME:

SCIENTIFIC NAME:

COMMON NAME: DATE:

LOCATION:

SCIENTIFIC NAME: HABITAT:

WEATHER:

SIZE/SEX:

REMARKS:

COMMON NAME: DATE:

LOCATION:

SCIENTIFIC NAME: HABITAT:

WEATHER:

SIZE/SEX:

REMARKS:

COMMON NAME: DATE:

LOCATION:

SCIENTIFIC NAME: HABITAT:

WEATHER:

SIZE/SEX:

REMARKS:

LEAFNOSE, SHOVELNOSE, AND BANDED SAND SNAKES

Family: Colubridae
Genera: *Phyllorhynchus, Chionactis,* and *Chilomeniscus*

THESE NOCTURNAL subterranean burrowers are strictly limited in range to the deserts and arid regions of the southwestern United States and northern Mexico. All are petite in size, ranging from the tiny banded sand snakes (7 to 10 inches long) to the shovelnose snakes (10 to 17 inches) and the leafnose snakes (12 to 20 inches). Species from these genera are "specialists" in desert survival and prosper in very harsh environments, often occurring in the most arid part of the desert. During warm weather, these species become strictly nocturnal. The leafnose snake (*Phyllorhynchus*) has a greatly enlarged rostral scale that helps it burrow in coarse soils. The lower jaw in both the shovelnose (*Chionactis*) and banded sand snakes (*Chilomeniscus*) is deeply inset, which also aids in burrowing. Shovelnose and banded sand snakes feed on insects, spiders, scorpions, centipedes, and ant pupae. Shovelnose snakes are at least partially immune to the venom of North American scorpions. Banded geckos (*Coleonyx*) are the main prey of leafnose snakes.

Pima Saddled Leafnose Snake
Phyllorhynchus browni browni

DATE:

LOCATION:

HABITAT:

WEATHER:

SIZE/SEX:

REMARKS:

Maricopa Saddled Leafnose Snake
Phyllorhynchus browni lucidus

DATE:

LOCATION:

HABITAT:

WEATHER:

SIZE/SEX:

REMARKS:

Clouded Leafnose Snake
Phyllorhynchus decurtatus nubilis

This is a subspecies of the Spotted Leafnose Snake.

DATE:

LOCATION:

HABITAT:

WEATHER:

SIZE/SEX:

REMARKS:

This is a subspecies of the Spotted Leafnose Snake.

Western Leafnose Snake
Phyllorhynchus decurtatus perkinsi

DATE:

LOCATION:

HABITAT:

WEATHER:

SIZE/SEX:

REMARKS:

This is a subspecies of the Western Shovelnose Snake.

Mojave Shovelnose Snake
Chionactis occipitalis occipitalis

DATE:

LOCATION:

HABITAT:

WEATHER:

SIZE/SEX:

REMARKS:

This is a subspecies of the Western Shovelnose Snake.

Colorado Desert Shovelnose Snake
Chionactis occipitalis annulata

DATE:

LOCATION:

HABITAT:

WEATHER:

SIZE/SEX:

REMARKS:

**Colorado Desert
Shovelnose Snake
(Anza-Borrego phase)**
*Chionactis occipitalis
annulata*

This morph, which lacks the red crossbands, is most commonly encountered in the area of Anza-Borrego Desert State Park, San Diego County, California.

DATE:

LOCATION:

HABITAT:

WEATHER:

SIZE/SEX:

REMARKS:

Tucson Shovelnose Snake
*Chionactis occipitalis
klauberi*

This is a subspecies of the Western Shovelnose Snake.

DATE:

LOCATION:

HABITAT:

WEATHER:

SIZE/SEX:

REMARKS:

Nevada Shovelnose Snake
*Chionactis occipitalis
talpina*

This is a subspecies of the Western Shovelnose Snake.

DATE:

LOCATION:

HABITAT:

WEATHER:

SIZE/SEX:

REMARKS:

This is a subspecies of the Sonoran Shovelnose Snake.

DATE:

LOCATION:

HABITAT:

WEATHER:

SIZE/SEX:

REMARKS:

Organ Pipe Shovelnose Snake
Chionactis palarostris organica

DATE:

LOCATION:

HABITAT:

WEATHER:

SIZE/SEX:

REMARKS:

Banded Sand Snake
Chilomeniscus cinctus

DATE:

LOCATION:

HABITAT:

WEATHER:

SIZE/SEX:

REMARKS:

Additional species, subspecies, and forms

COMMON NAME:

SCIENTIFIC NAME:

COMMON NAME: DATE:

LOCATION:

SCIENTIFIC NAME: HABITAT:

WEATHER:

SIZE/SEX:

REMARKS:

COMMON NAME: DATE:

LOCATION:

SCIENTIFIC NAME: HABITAT:

WEATHER:

SIZE/SEX:

REMARKS:

COMMON NAME: DATE:

LOCATION:

SCIENTIFIC NAME: HABITAT:

WEATHER:

SIZE/SEX:

REMARKS:

REAR-FANGED SNAKES
Night, Cat-eyed, Vine, Hooknose, Black-striped, Blackhead, and Lyre Snakes

Family: Colubridae
Genera: *Hypsiglena, Leptodeira, Oxybelis, Gyalopion, Ficimia, Coniophanes, Tantilla*, and *Trimorphodon*

THESE SNAKES are in different stages of the development of venom and venom apparatus. The genera *Gyalopion* and *Ficimia* (hooknose), *Tantilla* (blackhead), and *Hypsiglena* (night) either have not fully developed their venom or have not evolved a functional venom-delivery apparatus. The development of venom apparatus in these species is an evolutionary process that assists these snakes in subduing prey, usually lizards or insects.

The cat-eyed (*Leptodeira*), black-striped (*Coniophanes*), lyre (*Trimorphodon*), and vine (*Oxybelis*) snakes are more advanced and equipped with functional grooved fangs and venom but are not usually considered dangerous to humans. The vine snake, however, as well as large lyre and cat-eyed snakes, should be handled with caution. People bitten by these species have reported pain and swelling at the site of the bite.

Rear-fanged snakes found in the United States range in length from 5 inches (blackhead snakes) to 5 feet (vine snakes).

It should be noted that whereas most authorities recognize only one subspecies of night snakes found in the United States and refer to all as *Hypsiglena torquata torquata*, others recognize six distinct subspecies.

Desert Night Snake   DATE:

Hypsiglena torquata
deserticola   LOCATION:

STATUS: SENSITIVE, State   HABITAT:
of Idaho
                                      WEATHER:

                                      SIZE/SEX:

                                      REMARKS:

San Diego Night Snake   DATE:

Hypsiglena torquata
klauberi   LOCATION:

                                       HABITAT:

                                       WEATHER:

                                       SIZE/SEX:

                                       REMARKS:

Mesa Verde Night Snake   DATE:

Hypsiglena torquata loreala   LOCATION:

                                       HABITAT:

                                       WEATHER:

                                       SIZE/SEX:

                                       REMARKS:

DATE:

LOCATION:

HABITAT:

WEATHER:

SIZE/SEX:

REMARKS:

California Night Snake
Hypsiglena torquata nuchalata

DATE:

LOCATION:

HABITAT:

WEATHER:

SIZE/SEX:

REMARKS:

Texas Night Snake
Hypsiglena torquata jani

STATUS: THREATENED, State of Kansas
DO NOT COLLECT: PROTECTED SPECIES

DATE:

LOCATION:

HABITAT:

WEATHER:

SIZE/SEX:

REMARKS:

Spotted Night Snake
Hypsiglena torquata ochrorhyncha

Cat-eyed Snake
Leptodeira septentrionalis septentrionalis

STATUS: ENDANGERED, State of Texas
DO NOT COLLECT: PROTECTED SPECIES

DATE:

LOCATION:

HABITAT:

WEATHER:

SIZE/SEX:

REMARKS:

Brown Vine Snake
Oxybelis aeneus

STATUS: CANDIDATE, endangered or threatened species listing, State of Arizona

DATE:

LOCATION:

HABITAT:

WEATHER:

SIZE/SEX:

REMARKS

Thornscrub Hooknose Snake
Gyalopion quadrangularis desertorum

DATE:

LOCATION:

HABITAT:

WEATHER:

SIZE/SEX:

REMARKS:

DATE:

LOCATION:

HABITAT:

WEATHER:

SIZE/SEX:

REMARKS:

Chihuauhuan Hooknose Snake
Gyalopion canum

DATE:

LOCATION:

HABITAT:

WEATHER:

SIZE/SEX:

REMARKS:

Mexican Hooknose Snake
Ficimia streckeri

DATE:

LOCATION:

HABITAT:

WEATHER:

SIZE/SEX:

REMARKS:

Black-striped Snake
Coniophanes imperialis imperialis

STATUS: THREATENED, State of Texas
DO NOT COLLECT: PROTECTED SPECIES

California Blackhead Snake
Tantilla planiceps eiseni

DATE:

LOCATION:

HABITAT:

WEATHER:

SIZE/SEX:

REMARKS:

Huachuca Blackhead Snake
Tantilla wilcoxi wilcoxi

DATE:

LOCATION:

HABITAT:

WEATHER:

SIZE/SEX:

REMARKS:

Southwestern Blackhead Snake
Tantilla hobartsmithi

DATE:

LOCATION:

HABITAT:

WEATHER:

SIZE/SEX:

REMARKS:

DATE:

LOCATION:

HABITAT:

WEATHER:

SIZE/SEX:

REMARKS:

Plains Blackhead Snake
Tantilla nigriceps nigriceps

DATE:

LOCATION:

HABITAT:

WEATHER:

SIZE/SEX:

REMARKS:

Yaqui Blackhead Snake
Tantilla yaquia

DATE:

LOCATION:

HABITAT:

WEATHER:

SIZE/SEX:

REMARKS:

Mexican Blackhead Snake
Tantilla atriceps

Devil's River Blackhead Snake
Tantilla rubra diabola

DATE:

LOCATION:

HABITAT:

WEATHER:

SIZE/SEX:

REMARKS:

Blackhood Snake
Tantilla rubra cucullata

STATUS: THREATENED, State of Texas
DO NOT COLLECT: PROTECTED SPECIES

Pattern may be extremely variable throughout range.

DATE:

LOCATION:

HABITAT:

WEATHER:

SIZE/SEX:

REMARKS:

Desert Blackhead Snake
Tantilla planiceps transmontana

DATE:

LOCATION:

HABITAT:

WEATHER:

SIZE/SEX:

REMARKS:

DATE:

LOCATION:

HABITAT:

WEATHER:

SIZE/SEX:

REMARKS:

Utah Blackhead Snake
Tantilla planiceps utahensis

DATE:

LOCATION:

HABITAT:

WEATHER:

SIZE/SEX:

REMARKS:

Southeastern Crowned Snake
Tantilla coronata

STATUS: THREATENED, State of Indiana
DO NOT COLLECT: PROTECTED SPECIES

DATE:

LOCATION:

HABITAT:

WEATHER:

SIZE/SEX:

REMARKS:

Peninsula Crowned Snake
Tantilla relicta relicta

Central Florida Crowned Snake
Tantilla relicta neilli

DATE:

LOCATION:

HABITAT:

WEATHER:

SIZE/SEX:

REMARKS:

Coastal Dunes Crowned Snake
Tantilla relicta pamlica

DATE:

LOCATION:

HABITAT:

WEATHER:

SIZE/SEX:

REMARKS:

Rim Rock Crowned Snake
Tantilla oolitica

STATUS: THREATENED, State of Florida CANDIDATE, Federal endangered or threatened species listing
DO NOT COLLECT: PROTECTED SPECIES

DATE:

LOCATION:

HABITAT:

WEATHER:

SIZE/SEX:

REMARKS:

DATE:

LOCATION:

HABITAT:

WEATHER:

SIZE/SEX:

REMARKS:

Flathead Snake
Tantilla gracilis

DATE:

LOCATION:

HABITAT:

WEATHER:

SIZE/SEX:

REMARKS:

Texas Lyre Snake
Trimorphodon biscutatus vilkinsoni

STATUS: THREATENED, State of Texas
DO NOT COLLECT: PROTECTED SPECIES

Color may be somewhat variable throughout range.

DATE:

LOCATION:

HABITAT:

WEATHER:

SIZE/SEX:

REMARKS:

Sonoran Lyre Snake
Trimorphodon biscutatus lambda

STATUS: CANDIDATE, endangered or threatened species listing, State of Utah

California Lyre Snake
*Trimorphodon biscutatus
vandenburghi*

DATE:

LOCATION:

HABITAT:

WEATHER:

SIZE/SEX:

REMARKS:

**California Lyre Snake
(Pisgah color phase)**
*Trimorphodon biscutatus
vandenburghi*

This very dark morph has evolved in, and is restricted to, the area of the Pisgah Lava Flow, located in the Mojave Desert of California.

DATE:

LOCATION:

HABITAT:

WEATHER:

SIZE/SEX:

REMARKS:

**Additional species,
subspecies, and forms**

COMMON NAME:

SCIENTIFIC NAME:

DATE:

LOCATION:

HABITAT:

WEATHER:

SIZE/SEX:

REMARKS:

DATE: COMMON NAME:

LOCATION:

HABITAT: SCIENTIFIC NAME:

WEATHER:

SIZE/SEX:

REMARKS:

DATE: COMMON NAME:

LOCATION:

HABITAT: SCIENTIFIC NAME:

WEATHER:

SIZE/SEX:

REMARKS:

DATE: COMMON NAME:

LOCATION:

HABITAT: SCIENTIFIC NAME:

WEATHER:

SIZE/SEX:

REMARKS:

PIT VIPERS

Family: Viperidae
Subfamily: Crotalinae

MEMBERS OF this subfamily are found in both the Old World and the New. The group is represented in the United States by copperheads, cottonmouths, and rattlesnakes. These snakes have a deep facial pit on each side of the face, between the eye and nostril, hence the name. These pits are heat-sensing organs which assist the snakes in locating and striking at warm-blooded prey with exceptional accuracy. Any snake with such a pit is venomous. All pit vipers have vertically elliptical pupils (cat-eyed) and their heads are usually very distinct from their necks, often triangular in shape. These snakes have very well-developed venom delivery apparatus, which includes large, hollow fangs that unfold from the roof of the mouth when striking.

COPPERHEADS AND COTTONMOUTHS

Family: Viperidae
Genus: *Agkistrodon*

COPPERHEADS AND cottonmouths, although closely related, are quite different in several respects. Copperheads are medium-sized snakes averaging 2 to 3 feet in length with occasional individuals of the Northern or Southern species exceeding 4 feet. Cottonmouths are larger and more heavy bodied than copperheads; adult cottonmouths average 3 to 4 feet in length, while some specimens may exceed 6 feet. Copperheads are usually very attractive snakes with various hues of brown and gold, while cottonmouths (especially older snakes) are uniformly a dingy dark green, brown, or black. Copperheads are among the most reclusive of our snakes, usually preferring to lie in motionless camouflage on the leafy forest floor rather than assume a defensive striking position and reveal their presence. Because of this preference, and the snake's ordinarily mild disposition, copperheads generally do not pose a significant threat to the careful outdoorsman. Cottonmouths often display a very irritable disposition, standing their ground, holding the mouth open and displaying its white interior, hence the name "cottonmouth."

The preferred habitat of most copperhead subspecies is rocky, wooded hillsides where small rodents are abundant. In the case of the Northern, Osage, and Broad-banded copperheads, this habitat is often shared by the Timber Rattlesnake (*Crotalus horridus*). The Southern and Trans-Pecos subspecies are normally found in damper habitats, often in the vicinity of water. Cottonmouths, also called "water moccasins," are thoroughly aquatic and are at home in swamps, marshes, lakes, and ponds, and along rivers.

Although human fatalities have been recorded from the bites of both copperheads and cottonmouths, the cottonmouth is by far the more dangerous of the two due to its larger size, venom capacity, and its often foul temperament. Small rodents make up the main part of the copperhead's diet, while cottonmouths prey chiefly on fish and amphibians. The young of both copperheads and cottonmouths have a bright yellow- or greenish yellow-tipped tail that is used for attracting prey, often frogs.

Northern Copperhead
*Agkistrodon contortrix
mokeson*

STATUS: ENDANGERED,
states of Massachusetts
and Iowa
WATCHLIST SPECIES,
State of New York
**DO NOT COLLECT:
PROTECTED SPECIES**

DATE:

LOCATION:

HABITAT:

WEATHER:

SIZE/SEX:

REMARKS:

Southern Copperhead
*Agkistrodon contortrix
contortrix*

STATUS: ENDANGERED,
State of Iowa
**DO NOT COLLECT:
PROTECTED SPECIES**

DATE:

LOCATION:

HABITAT:

WEATHER:

SIZE/SEX:

REMARKS

Osage Copperhead
*Agkistrodon contortrix
phaeogaster*

STATUS: ENDANGERED,
State of Iowa
**DO NOT COLLECT:
PROTECTED SPECIES**

DATE:

LOCATION:

HABITAT:

WEATHER:

SIZE/SEX:

REMARKS:

Some individuals have been found with very slight crossband traces or no crossbands at all, uniformly light tan in color. This form differs dramatically from the norm.

DATE:

LOCATION:

HABITAT:

WEATHER:

SIZE/SEX:

REMARKS:

Osage Copperhead (patternless phase)
Agkistrodon contortrix phaeogaster

STATUS: ENDANGERED, State of Iowa
DO NOT COLLECT: PROTECTED SPECIES

DATE:

LOCATION:

HABITAT:

WEATHER:

SIZE/SEX:

REMARKS:

Broad-banded Copperhead
Agkistrodon contortrix laticinctus

DATE:

LOCATION:

HABITAT:

WEATHER:

SIZE/SEX:

REMARKS:

Trans-Pecos Copperhead
Agkistrodon contortrix pictigaster

Eastern Cottonmouth
Agkistrodon piscivorus piscivorus

Pattern and/or color may be somewhat variable throughout range.

DATE:

LOCATION:

HABITAT:

WEATHER:

SIZE/SEX:

REMARKS:

Florida Cottonmouth
Agkistrodon piscivorus conanti

Pattern and/or color may be somewhat variable throughout range.

DATE:

LOCATION:

HABITAT:

WEATHER:

SIZE/SEX:

REMARKS:

Western Cottonmouth
Agkistrodon piscivorus leucostoma

STATUS: THREATENED, State of Indiana
DO NOT COLLECT: PROTECTED SPECIES

Pattern and/or color may be somewhat variable throughout range.

DATE:

LOCATION:

HABITAT:

WEATHER:

SIZE/SEX:

REMARKS:

DATE:

LOCATION:

HABITAT:

WEATHER:

SIZE/SEX:

REMARKS:

Additional species, subspecies, and forms

COMMON NAME:

SCIENTIFIC NAME:

DATE:

LOCATION:

HABITAT:

WEATHER:

SIZE/SEX:

REMARKS:

COMMON NAME:

SCIENTIFIC NAME:

DATE:

LOCATION:

HABITAT:

WEATHER:

SIZE/SEX:

REMARKS:

COMMON NAME:

SCIENTIFIC NAME:

RATTLESNAKES

Family: Viperidae
Genera: *Crotalus* and *Sistrurus*

AT LEAST one species of rattlesnake is found in each of the forty-eight contiguous states with the exceptions of Maine and Delaware. The greatest numbers of rattlesnakes, in terms both of variety and of abundance, are found in the southwestern United States. Arizona ranks first with eighteen species and subspecies. The rattlesnake group comprises two genera: *Crotalus* and *Sistrurus*. Snakes of the genus *Crotalus* are generally the larger of the two, with one species occasionally exceeding 8 feet in length. Snakes of this genus have a mixture of large and small scales on the crown. Members of the genus *Sistrurus* have a group of 9 large scales on the crown and are quite small, rarely exceeding 30 inches in length.

Like the copperheads and cottonmouths, rattlesnakes are pit vipers. Several rattlesnake species are considered extremely dangerous due to their size, disposition, and/or the potency of their venom. These species include the Eastern and Western diamondback rattlesnakes, which are responsible for more fatalities than any other snakes in the United States, and the Mojave Rattlesnake, which generally has the most potent venom (drop for drop). The great majority of rattlesnake bites occur after someone intentionally interacts with the snake by attempting to capture or kill it. In the United States, the rattlesnake is by far the most persecuted of our snakes. Many species of rattlers are now much less common than they were, and some are completely extirpated from much of their historical range due to habitat destruction, human encroachment into formerly wild areas, extermination of denning areas, and other human crusades such as rattlesnake roundups, which still occur legally in several states.

Rattlesnakes are a very important, integral part of our ecosystems, as both predator and prey. Crop-destructive rodents make up the principal diet for many of our larger species of rattlesnakes, making them very beneficial to farmers and ranchers. Rattlers are preyed upon by a large number of animals, including roadrunners, hawks, owls, many mammal species including javelinas, badgers, foxes, skunks, and weasels, and other reptile and amphibian species including kingsnakes, indigo snakes, alligators, and even bullfrogs. Humans are without a doubt the rattlesnake's worst enemy. When found in the wild away from human habitation, rattlesnakes should never be killed.

Rattlesnakes are generally not aggressive; they will coil in a defensive posture, stand their ground, and rattle, but *will not* attack humans unless provoked. The very small percentage of rattlesnake bites that are not the result of human attempts to interact with the animal usually occur after someone steps on the snake or puts a hand or foot in such close proximity that the snake perceives a threat. It may sound simplistic to make this statement, but I find people tend to forget that their size alone is intimidating to a smaller species. Persuading people not to kill rattlesnakes on sight, however, is not easy when they have, been told for their entire lives, and wholeheartedly believe, that "the only good rattlesnake is a dead rattlesnake."

In the author's opinion, the existence as a species of this magnificent creature is threatened throughout its entire range. This species, which on occasion exceeds 8 feet in length, is the heaviest venomous snake on earth and, as an adult, is at or near the top of the food chain wherever it is found. Like other large predators, the Eastern Diamondback needs large tracts of wilderness to survive, and because this impressive species lives in the "sunbelt," it is quickly losing in competition with the multitudes of humans who also choose to call these subtropical rattlesnake habitats their home. Let us hope that this species can be saved for future generations to appreciate and respect.

Eastern Diamondback Rattlesnake
Crotalus adamanteus

STATUS: ENDANGERED, State of Louisiana (considered critically imperiled in this state and especially vulnerable to extirpation.)
DO NOT COLLECT: PROTECTED SPECIES

DATE:

LOCATION:

HABITAT:

WEATHER:

SIZE/SEX:

REMARKS:

**Western Diamondback
Rattlesnake**
Crotalus atrox atrox

DATE:

LOCATION:

HABITAT:

WEATHER:

SIZE/SEX:

REMARKS:

**Western Diamondback
Rattlesnake (dark phase)**
Crotalus atrox atrox

Very dark individuals, some nearly black, have been found on the Almendariz lava flows in Socorro and Sierra counties in central New Mexico.

DATE:

LOCATION:

HABITAT:

WEATHER:

SIZE/SEX:

REMARKS:

**Western Diamondback
Rattlesnake (reddish
brown phase)**
Crotalus atrox atrox

This morph, which closely resembles *Crotalus ruber,* occurs sporadically throughout a wide range; however it is most often encountered in the Sulphur Springs and San Simon valleys of southeastern Arizona.

DATE:

LOCATION:

HABITAT:

WEATHER:

SIZE/SEX:

REMARKS:

DATE:

LOCATION:

HABITAT:

WEATHER:

SIZE/SEX:

REMARKS:

Red Diamond Rattlesnake
Crotalus ruber

STATUS: CANDIDATE, Federal endangered or threatened species listing

---

Color may be extremely varied throughout range.

DATE:

LOCATION:

HABITAT:

WEATHER:

SIZE/SEX:

REMARKS:

Southwestern Speckled Rattlesnake
Crotalus mitchellii pyrrhus

STATUS: CANDIDATE, endangered or threatened species listing, State of Utah

---

Very dark, nearly black, individuals have been found at Pisgah lava flow, San Bernardino County, California.

DATE:

LOCATION:

HABITAT:

WEATHER:

SIZE/SEX:

REMARKS:

Southwestern Speckled Rattlesnake (dark phase)
Crotalus mitchellii pyrrhus

STATUS: CANDIDATE, endangered or threatened species listing, State of Utah

Panamint Speckled Rattlesnake, Panamint Rattlesnake
Crotalus mitchellii stephensi

DATE:

LOCATION:

HABITAT:

WEATHER:

SIZE/SEX:

REMARKS:

Banded Rock Rattlesnake (bluish gray phase)
Crotalus lepidus klauberi

STATUS: PROTECTED SPECIES, State of Arizona
DO NOT COLLECT: PROTECTED SPECIES

Surveys of Banded Rock Rattlesnake populations have revealed that this form often demonstrates sexual dimorphism in which the majority of males are greenish, while the majority of females are bluish gray. The two morphs are given separate entries here.

DATE:

LOCATION:

HABITAT:

WEATHER:

SIZE/SEX:

REMARKS:

Banded Rock Rattlesnake (greenish phase)
Crotalus lepidus klauberi

STATUS: PROTECTED SPECIES, State of Arizona
DO NOT COLLECT: PROTECTED SPECIES

DATE:

LOCATION:

HABITAT:

WEATHER:

SIZE/SEX:

REMARKS:

The Mottled Rock Rattlesnake can be extremely variable in color and somewhat variable in pattern. Approximately forty distinct variations have been recorded, ranging from nearly plain white with no pattern, to nearly black, to bright orange. It is interesting to note that the ground color of these cryptic snakes usually mimics the color of surrounding rock formations. The first two phases listed are the most commonly observed morphs.

DATE:

LOCATION:

HABITAT:

WEATHER:

SIZE/SEX:

REMARKS:

Mottled Rock Rattlesnake (reddish phase)
Crotalus lepidus lepidus

STATUS: ENDANGERED, State of New Mexico, Group 2
DO NOT COLLECT: PROTECTED SPECIES

DATE:

LOCATION:

HABITAT:

WEATHER:

SIZE/SEX:

REMARKS:

Mottled Rock Rattlesnake (grayish phase)
Crotalus lepidus lepidus

STATUS: ENDANGERED, State of New Mexico, Group 2
DO NOT COLLECT: PROTECTED SPECIES

Mottled Rock Rattlesnake (patternless phase)
Crotalus lepidus lepidus

STATUS: ENDANGERED, State of New Mexico, Group 2
DO NOT COLLECT: PROTECTED SPECIES

Some individuals encountered in the field have little or no trace of any pattern and are quite stunning.

DATE:

LOCATION:

HABITAT:

WEATHER:

SIZE/SEX:

REMARKS:

Mojave Desert Sidewinder
Crotalus cerastes cerastes

STATUS: CANDIDATE, endangered or threatened species listing, State of Utah

DATE:

LOCATION:

HABITAT:

WEATHER:

SIZE/SEX:

REMARKS:

Sonoran Desert Sidewinder
Crotalus cerastes cercobombus

DATE:

LOCATION:

HABITAT:

WEATHER:

SIZE/SEX:

REMARKS:

DATE:

LOCATION:

HABITAT:

WEATHER:

SIZE/SEX:

REMARKS:

Colorado Desert Sidewinder
Crotalus cerastes laterorepens

The color of these usually docile rattlers can be quite variable. It should be noted that Texas Blacktails are usually greenish gray, while the snakes from the highlands of Arizona are often a beautiful, bright golden color.

DATE:

LOCATION:

HABITAT:

WEATHER:

SIZE/SEX:

REMARKS:

Northern Blacktail Rattlesnake
Crotalus molossus molossus

Very dark, nearly black, individuals have been found on lava flows at several locations in New Mexico and Arizona.

DATE:

LOCATION:

HABITAT:

WEATHER:

SIZE/SEX:

REMARKS:

Northern Blacktail Rattlesnake (dark phase)
Crotalus molossus molossus

Tiger Rattlesnake
Crotalus tigris

Color may be somewhat varied throughout range.

DATE:

LOCATION:

HABITAT:

WEATHER:

SIZE/SEX:

REMARKS:

Mojave Rattlesnake
Crotalus scutulatus scutulatus

STATUS: CANDIDATE, endangered or threatened species listing, State of Utah

Pattern and/or color may be somewhat variable throughout range.

DATE:

LOCATION:

HABITAT:

WEATHER:

SIZE/SEX:

REMARKS:

Mojave Rattlesnake (striped phase)
Crotalus scutulatus scutulatus

Several Mojaves encountered in southern Arizona have had stripes running from the head approximately one-quarter the length of the snake, closely resembling Tropical Rattlesnakes (*Crotalus durissus* sp.).

DATE:

LOCATION:

HABITAT:

WEATHER:

SIZE/SEX:

REMARKS:

DATE:

LOCATION:

HABITAT:

WEATHER:

SIZE/SEX:

REMARKS:

Prairie Rattlesnake
Crotalus viridis viridis

STATUS: ENDANGERED,
State of Iowa
**DO NOT COLLECT:
PROTECTED SPECIES**

DATE:

LOCATION:

HABITAT:

WEATHER:

SIZE/SEX:

REMARKS:

Great Basin Rattlesnake
Crotalus viridis lutosus

DATE:

LOCATION:

HABITAT:

WEATHER:

SIZE/SEX:

REMARKS:

**Arizona Black
Rattlesnake**
Crotalus viridis cerberus

**Grand Canyon
Rattlesnake**
Crotalus viridis abyssus

STATUS: See above.

This beautiful pink or salmon-colored subspecies of the Western Rattlesnake is limited in distribution to the floor and lower elevations of the Grand Canyon in Arizona. It is not found outside Grand Canyon National Park and small portions of adjacent Indian lands, and is protected in all areas where it occurs. It is, therefore, illegal to collect the Grand Canyon Rattlesnake.

DATE:

LOCATION:

HABITAT:

WEATHER:

SIZE/SEX:

REMARKS:

Midget Faded Rattlesnake
Crotalus viridis concolor

STATUS: PROTECTED,
State of Colorado
**DO NOT COLLECT:
PROTECTED SPECIES**

DATE:

LOCATION:

HABITAT:

WEATHER:

SIZE/SEX:

REMARKS:

**Southern Pacific
Rattlesnake**
Crotalus viridis helleri

DATE:

LOCATION:

HABITAT:

WEATHER:

SIZE/SEX:

REMARKS:

DATE:

LOCATION:

HABITAT:

WEATHER:

SIZE/SEX:

REMARKS:

Northern Pacific Rattlesnake
Crotalus viridis oreganus

DATE:

LOCATION:

HABITAT:

WEATHER:

SIZE/SEX:

REMARKS:

Hopi Rattlesnake
Crotalus viridis nuntius

**Timber Rattlesnake
(dark phase)**
Crotalus horridus horridus

STATUS: EXTIRPATED or
EXTINCT, State of Maine
ENDANGERED, states of
Massachusetts, Vermont,
Connecticut, Rhode Is-
land, New Hampshire,
and New Jersey
THREATENED, states of
Texas, New York, and
Indiana
SPECIES OF SPECIAL
CONCERN, State of
Minnesota
CANDIDATE, endan-
gered or threatened spe-
cies listing; State of
Pennsylvania
**DO NOT COLLECT:
PROTECTED SPECIES**

DATE:

LOCATION:

HABITAT:

WEATHER:

SIZE/SEX:

REMARKS:

**Timber Rattlesnake
(light phase)**
Crotalus horridus horridus

STATUS: EXTIRPATED or
EXTINCT, State of Maine
ENDANGERED, states of
Massachusetts, Vermont,
Connecticut, Rhode Is-
land, New Hampshire,
and New Jersey
THREATENED, states of
Texas, New York, and
Indiana
SPECIES OF SPECIAL
CONCERN, State of
Minnesota
CANDIDATE, endan-
gered or threatened spe-
cies listing; State of
Pennsylvania
**DO NOT COLLECT:
PROTECTED SPECIES**

DATE:

LOCATION:

HABITAT:

WEATHER:

SIZE/SEX:

REMARKS:

The canebrake form is now considered a regional color phase of *Crotalus horridus horridus* by many. Unlike the typical "timber rattler," this form, which has a reddish brown middorsal stripe, is at home in the lowlands of the southeastern coastal plain.

DATE:

LOCATION:

HABITAT:

WEATHER:

SIZE/SEX:

REMARKS:

Timber Rattlesnake (canebrake phase)
Crotalus horridus atricaudatus

STATUS: ENDANGERED, State of Virginia
DO NOT COLLECT: PROTECTED SPECIES

This morph closely resembles the canebrake phase in having a reddish middorsal stripe. The dark crossbands are usually edged in white. This phase is generally found west of the Mississippi River and north of the Ozark Mountains, including Iowa, Missouri, Nebraska, Kansas, Wisconsin, and Minnesota.

DATE:

LOCATION:

HABITAT:

WEATHER:

SIZE/SEX:

REMARKS:

Timber Rattlesnake (western phase)
Crotalus horridus horridus

STATUS: EXTIRPATED or EXTINCT, State of Maine
ENDANGERED, states of Massachusetts, Vermont, Connecticut, Rhode Island, New Hampshire, and New Jersey
THREATENED, states of Texas, New York, and Indiana
SPECIES OF SPECIAL CONCERN, State of Minnesota
CANDIDATE, endangered or threatened species listing, State of Pennsylvania
DO NOT COLLECT: PROTECTED SPECIES

Western Twin-spotted Rattlesnake
Crotalus pricei pricei

STATUS: PROTECTED SPECIES, State of Arizona
DO NOT COLLECT: PROTECTED SPECIES

DATE:

LOCATION:

HABITAT:

WEATHER:

SIZE/SEX:

REMARKS:

Arizona Ridgenose Rattlesnake
Crotalus willardi willardi

STATUS: PROTECTED SPECIES, State of Arizona
DO NOT COLLECT: PROTECTED SPECIES

DATE:

LOCATION:

HABITAT:

WEATHER:

SIZE/SEX:

REMARKS:

Animas Ridgenose Rattlesnake
Crotalus willardi obscurus

STATUS: ENDANGERED, State of New Mexico, Group 1
THREATENED, Federal
PROTECTED, State of Arizona
DO NOT COLLECT: PROTECTED SPECIES

DATE:

LOCATION:

HABITAT:

WEATHER:

SIZE/SEX:

REMARKS:

DATE:

LOCATION:

HABITAT:

WEATHER:

SIZE/SEX:

REMARKS:

Eastern Massasauga
Sistrurus catenatus catenatus

STATUS: ENDANGERED, states of Pennsylvania, Wisconsin, New York, Iowa, and Missouri THREATENED, State of Indiana SPECIES OF SPECIAL CONCERN, State of Minnesota CANDIDATE, Federal endangered or threatened species listing **DO NOT COLLECT: PROTECTED SPECIES**

Individuals found in some locations are nearly all black above and below with little or no pattern.

DATE:

LOCATION:

HABITAT:

WEATHER:

SIZE/SEX:

REMARKS:

Eastern Massasauga (black phase)
Sistrurus catenatus catenatus

STATUS: ENDANGERED, states of Pennsylvania, Wisconsin, New York, Iowa, and Missouri THREATENED, State of Indiana SPECIES OF SPECIAL CONCERN, State of Minnesota CANDIDATE, Federal endangered or threatened species listing **DO NOT COLLECT: PROTECTED SPECIES**

Western Massasauga
Sistrurus catenatus tergeminus

STATUS: ENDANGERED, State of Missouri
DO NOT COLLECT: PROTECTED SPECIES

DATE:

LOCATION:

HABITAT:

WEATHER:

SIZE/SEX:

REMARKS:

Desert Grassland Massasauga
Sistrurus catenatus edwardsi

STATUS: ENDANGERED, State of Arizona
PROTECTED, State of Colorado
SPECIES OF SPECIAL CONCERN, State of Oklahoma
DO NOT COLLECT: PROTECTED SPECIES

DATE:

LOCATION:

HABITAT:

WEATHER:

SIZE/SEX:

REMARKS:

Carolina Pigmy Rattlesnake
Sistrurus miliarius miliarius

STATUS: PROTECTED, State of North Carolina
DO NOT COLLECT: PROTECTED SPECIES

DATE:

LOCATION:

HABITAT:

WEATHER:

SIZE/SEX:

REMARKS:

This attractive morph, which displays various shades of red or orange, is found in a very limited area near Lake Mattamuskeet, North Carolina, where it receives protection under North Carolina law. Because of its unique appearance, it has suffered by poaching from unscrupulous collectors.

DATE:

LOCATION:

HABITAT:

WEATHER:

SIZE/SEX:

REMARKS:

Carolina Pigmy Rattlesnake (Mattamuskeet or red phase)
Sistrurus miliarius miliarius

STATUS: Protected, State of North Carolina
DO NOT COLLECT: PROTECTED SPECIES

This attractive purplish morph is largely restricted to the "sandhills" region of Moore County, North Carolina. Like the Mattumuskeet phase, this unusual color phase is often collected illegally.

DATE:

LOCATION:

HABITAT:

SIZE/SEX:

REMARKS:

Carolina Pigmy Rattlesnake (lavender phase)
Sistrurus miliarius miliarius

STATUS: PROTECTED, State of North Carolina
DO NOT COLLECT: PROTECTED SPECIES

DATE:

LOCATION:

HABITAT:

WEATHER:

SIZE/SEX:

REMARKS:

Dusky Pigmy Rattlesnake
Sistrurus miliarius barbouri

Western Pigmy Rattlesnake
Sistrurus miliarius streckeri

STATUS: THREATENED, states of Tennessee and Kentucky
DO NOT COLLECT: PROTECTED SPECIES

DATE:

LOCATION:

HABITAT:

WEATHER:

SIZE/SEX:

REMARKS:

Additional species, subspecies, and forms

COMMON NAME:

SCIENTIFIC NAME:

DATE:

LOCATION:

HABITAT:

WEATHER:

SIZE/SEX:

REMARKS:

COMMON NAME:

SCIENTIFIC NAME:

DATE:

LOCATION:

HABITAT:

WEATHER:

SIZE/SEX:

REMARKS:

DATE: COMMON NAME:

LOCATION:

HABITAT: SCIENTIFIC NAME:

WEATHER:

SIZE/SEX:

REMARKS:

DATE: COMMON NAME:

LOCATION:

HABITAT: SCIENTIFIC NAME:

WEATHER:

SIZE/SEX:

REMARKS:

DATE: COMMON NAME:

LOCATION:

HABITAT: SCIENTIFIC NAME:

WEATHER:

SIZE/SEX:

REMARKS:

CORAL SNAKES

Family: Elapidae
Genera: *Micrurus* and *Micruroides*

CORAL SNAKES belong to the same family of deadly snakes that includes such Old World allies as cobras, kraits, mambas, and Australian tiger snakes. They are unequivocally, drop for drop, the most venomous of American snakes but are among our least dangerous poisonous snakes. Humans are rarely bitten by coral snakes in the United States due to the serpent's usually docile temperament, secretive habits, small size, and inefficient biting apparatus. Most instances of humans bitten by coral snakes are a result of handling. Unlike pit vipers' defensive apparatus, which is generally designed to strike and release their prey, coral snakes' heads and short fangs are designed for seizing and holding prey. The Eastern and Texas coral snakes occasionally reach lengths in excess of 3½ feet, while the Arizona Coral Snake rarely exceeds 20 inches.

As with other members of the Elapidae family, the venom of the coral snake is to a large degree neurotoxic in composition, attacking the central nervous system. Interestingly, the venom of the Arizona Coral Snake, although still very potent, is much less toxic than that of the Eastern or Texas coral snakes. For that reason, and also because of the small size of the Arizona Coral Snake, no deaths have been recorded from the bite of this species.

Coral snakes feed largely on other snakes and lizards.

DATE:

LOCATION:

HABITAT:

WEATHER:

SIZE/SEX:

REMARKS:

Eastern Coral Snake
Micrurus fulvius fulvius

DATE:

LOCATION:

HABITAT:

WEATHER:

SIZE/SEX:

REMARKS:

Texas Coral Snake
Micrurus fulvius tener

This morph, found in the hammocks of the Everglades of Dade County, Florida, was at one time considered a distinct subspecies. It is now considered a regional color phase of the Eastern Coral Snake. There is usually a complete absence of black pigmentation on the red bands in this form.

South Florida Coral Snake
Micrurus fulvius barbouri

DATE:

LOCATION:

HABITAT:

WEATHER:

SIZE/SEX:

REMARKS:

Arizona Coral Snake
Micruroides euryxanthus euryxanthus

DATE:

LOCATION:

HABITAT:

WEATHER:

SIZE/SEX:

REMARKS:

Additional species, subspecies, and forms

COMMON NAME:

SCIENTIFIC NAME:

DATE:

LOCATION:

HABITAT:

WEATHER:

SIZE/SEX:

REMARKS:

COMMON NAME:

SCIENTIFIC NAME:

DATE:

LOCATION:

HABITAT:

WEATHER:

SIZE/SEX:

REMARKS:

SEA SNAKES

Family: Hydrophiidae
Genus: *Pelamis*

THE FAMILY *Hydrophiidae* contains two subfamilies, sixteen genera, and nearly sixty species of the world's most aquatic snakes endemic to the Pacific and Indian oceans. Sea snakes are believed to be closely akin to the family Elapidae.

Only one species of these oceanic snakes has been recorded in waters of the United States. They are truly aquatic and quite helpless on land; the tail is flattened and is used to propel them through the water when swimming or diving. Sea snakes are equipped with an organ in the mouth that helps to prevent excessive salt from entering the bloodstream.

Sea snakes are not found in the Atlantic Ocean; their rare occurrence in the continental United States has been limited to the waters off the coast of Southern California; they have also been reported in the waters of Hawaii. Worldwide, Yellow-bellied Sea Snakes are the most widely distributed of all snake species, with the possible exception of the Brown Tree Snake (*Boiga*). Yellow-bellied Sea Snakes are quite venomous but not usually aggressive. They are not large, averaging approximately 3 feet in length.

Yellow-bellied Sea Snake DATE:
Pelamis platurus

LOCATION:

HABITAT:

WEATHER:

SIZE/SEX:

REMARKS:

Additional species, DATE:
subspecies, and forms

LOCATION:

COMMON NAME:

HABITAT:

WEATHER:

SCIENTIFIC NAME:

SIZE/SEX:

REMARKS:

COMMON NAME: DATE:

LOCATION:

SCIENTIFIC NAME: HABITAT:

WEATHER:

SIZE/SEX:

REMARKS:

GLOSSARY

anal plate (n): an elongated scale, single or paired, lying just in front of the anus or vent.

anal spur (n): vestigial limbs of boids in the form of horny, pointed projections, one on each side, just above the vent.

amphiuma (n): a large, eel-like aquatic salamander native to the freshwater swamps and bayous of the southeastern and south central United States.

anerythristic (adj): melanistic.

aquatic (adj): frequenting water; living or growing in water.

arboreal (adj): adapted for living or climbing in trees.

azygous scale (n): a scale, usually on the midline and interposed between the paired scales on the top of the head.

cloaca (n): the common chamber into which, in reptiles and amphibians, the reproductive, intestinal, and urinary ducts open. The external opening of the cloaca is the vent or anus.

crepuscular (adj): active during twilight hours (dawn and dusk).

cryptic (adj): tending to remain concealed or camouflaged.

diurnal (adj): active by day.

dorsal (adj): relating to the back.

elliptical pupil (n): a vertical pupil, shaped much like the pupil of a cat. Genera native to the United States and Canada having vertically elliptical pupils include Agkistrodon, Charina, Crotalus, Hypsiglena, Leptodeira, Lichanura, Phyllorhynchus, Sistrurus, and Trimorphodon.

form (n): a species or subspecies; a distinct, identifiable population.

fossorial (adj): adapted for burrowing and digging.

gravid (adj): bearing eggs or young, usually in the oviducts; pregnant.

hammock (n): a tract of forested land elevated above the level of an adjacent marsh or swamp.

hybrid (n): offspring of two different species or genera.

intergrade (n): an intermediate form exhibiting a combination of characteristics of two or more subspecies

internasal (adj): of a plate or plates on the top of the head between the plates which surround the nostrils.

labial (adj): of the lips; usually refers to the scales bordering the lips.

melanism (adj): an abundance of black pigmentation, sometimes resulting in an all black or nearly all black animal.

middorsal (adj):   pertaining to the center of the back.

morph (n):   a distinct, identifiable population.

neurotoxic (adj):   damaging to the nervous system and neuromuscular function.

nocturnal (adj):   active by night.

ophiophague (n):   snake-eater.

oviparous (adj):   egg-bearing; producing eggs that hatch outside the body.

ovoviviparous (adj):   producing living young which have developed usually in the oviduct, with little or no connection between the foetus and mother.

phase (n):   a distinct, identifiable population.

prefrontal (adj):   of one or more scales on the top of the head lying immediately in front of the frontal shield.

race (n):   subspecies

reticulated (adj):   forming a network-like pattern.

riparian habitat (n):   a habitat adjacent to a river, stream, lake, pond, spring, seep, or other permanent body of water.

rostral scale (n):   the scale covering the tip of the snout, often enlarged in burrowing species.

sexual dimorphism (n):   marked differences in the shape, color, size, etc., between male and female of a species or subspecies.

siren (n):   a large aquatic salamander shaped like an eel but possessing external gills and forelegs.

sky islands (n):   a term used to describe forested mountain ranges of significant elevation that rise above desert areas. Regarded as islands in a sea of desert, these mountain ranges support habitats and species different from those in the desert below.

species (n):   a category of taxonomic classification ranking after genus and consisting of organisms capable of interbreeding.

subspecies (n):   a category of taxonomic classification ranking after species and usually based on a geographical distribution.

terrestrial (adj):   adapted for living on land; usually not arboreal or aquatic.

vent (n):   opening of the cloaca in reptiles and amphibians.

viviparous (adj):   live-bearing.

HERPETOLOGICAL ASSOCIATIONS AND UNIVERSITIES

FOR THOSE who are interested in meeting others with an interest in herpetology, a list of national and international herpetological societies and related organizations has been provided. A list of colleges and universities that offer degree programs or courses in herpetology has also been provided.

Alaska

Fairbanks Herpetocultural
  Society
P.O. Box 71309
Fairbanks, AK 99707
(907) 452-5400

Arizona

Arizona Herpetological
  Association
P.O. Box 39127
Phoenix, AZ 85069-9127
(602) 273-6445

International Society for the
  Study of Dendrobatid Frogs
2320 W. Palomino Dr.
Chandler, AZ 85224

International Venomous Snake
  Society
P.O. Box 4498
Apache Junction, AZ 85278-4498
(602) 987-6017

International Reptile and
  Amphibian Society
P.O. Box 876
Glendale, AZ 85311-0876
(602) 843-2024

Southern Arizona Herpetological
  Society
4521 W. Mars St.
Tucson, AZ 85703

National Turtle and Tortoise
  Society
P.O. Box 9806
Phoenix, AZ 85068-9806

Tucson Herpetological Society
P.O. Box 31531
Tucson, AZ 85751-1531

Arkansas

Arkansas Herpetological
  Association
418 N. Fairbanks
Russellville, AR 72801
(501) 968-6804

California

Bay Area Amphibian and Reptile
  Society
Palo Alto Junior Museum
1451 Middlefield Rd.
Palo Alto, CA 94301

California Turtle and Tortoise
  Society

Westchester Chapter
P.O. Box 90252
Los Angeles, CA 90009

Turtle and Tortoise Care
  Chapter
P.O. Box 2932
Santa Fe Springs, CA 90670

Foothill Chapter
P.O. Box 51002
Pasadena, CA 91115-1002

Valley Chapter
P.O. Box 44152
Panorama City, CA 91402

Executive Board
P.O. Box 7300
Van Nuys, CA 91409-7300

High Desert Chapter
P.O. Box 163
Victorville, CA 92392

Inland Empire Chapter
P.O. Box 2371
San Bernardino, CA 92406

Orange County Chapter
P.O. Box 11124
Santa Ana, CA 92711

Santa Barbara Chapter
P.O. Box 60745
Santa Barbara, CA 93160

TOOSLO Chapter
P.O. Box 14222
San Luis Obispo, CA 93406

Horned Lizard Conservation
  Society of Southern California
16377 Rancherias Rd.
Apple Valley, CA 92307
(619) 242-3370

Desert Tortoise Preserve
  Committee
P.O. Box 453
Ridgecrest, CA 93555

Inland Empire Herpetological
  Society
San Bernardino County Museum
2024 Orange Tree Ln.
Redlands, CA 92373

International Gecko Society
P.O. Box 370423
San Diego, CA 92137-0423

Kern County Herpetological
  Society
P.O. Box 762
Lebec, CA 93243-0762

North Bay Herpetological
  Society
6366 Commerce Blvd. #216
Rohnert Park, CA 94928

Northern California
  Herpetological Society
P.O. Box 1363
Davis, CA 95616-1363

Sacramento Turtle and Tortoise
  Club
25 Starlit Circle
Sacramento, CA 95831
(916) 421-1134

San Diego Herpetological Society
P.O. Box 4036
San Diego, CA 92164-4036
(619) 689-2582

San Diego Turtle and Tortoise
  Society
13963 Lyons Valley Rd.
Jamul, CA 92035

Chameleon Information
  Network
13419 Appalachian Way
San Diego, CA 92129
(619) 436-7978

San Joaquin Herpetological
  Society
P.O. Box 1104
Clovis, CA 93612-1104

Sea Turtle Center
P.O. Box 634
Nevada City, CA 95959

Shasta Snake Society
P.O. Box 171
Douglas City, CA 96024

Southern California Herpetology
  Association
P.O. Box 2932
Santa Fe Springs, CA 90670

Southwestern Herpetologists
  Society
P.O. Box 7469
Van Nuys, CA 91409

Turtle and Tortoise Education
  Adoption Media
3245 Military Ave.
Los Angeles, CA 90034

Varanid Information Exchange
8726D S. Sepulveda Blvd., #243
Los Angeles, CA 90045
(310) 768-8669

Colorado

Colorado Herpetological Society
P.O. Box 15381
Denver, CO 80215

Northeast Colorado
  Herpetological Society
6247 W. 10th St.
Greeley, CO 80361

Connecticut

Southern New England
  Herpetological Association
470 Durham Rd.
Madison, CT 06443-2060

Delaware

Delaware Herpetological Society
Ashland Nature Center
Brackenville and Barley Mill Rd.
Hockessin, DE 10707

Endangered Turtle Protection
  Foundation
P.O. Box 4617
Greenville, DE 19807

Florida

American Society of
  Ichthyologists and
  Herpetologists
Florida State Museum
University of Florida
Gainesville, FL 32611

Caribbean Conservation Corp.
P.O. Box 2866
Gainesville, FL 32606-2866

Central Florida Herpetological
  Society
P.O. Box 3277
Winter Haven, FL 33881
(813) 294-2235

Everglades Herpetological
  Society
6706 N.W. 169 St. Apt. A-108
Hialeah, FL 33015

Florida Marine Conservatory
274 Margaret St.
Key West, FL 33040

Florida Panhandle Herpetological
  Society
The Zoo
5801 Gulf Breeze Pkwy.
Gulf Breeze, FL 32561

Florida West Coast
  Herpetological and
  Conservation Society
P.O. Box 2725
Dunedin, FL 32526

Gainesville Herpetological
  Society
P.O. Box 140353
Gainesville, FL 32614-0353

Gopher Tortoise Council
611 NW 79 Dr.
Gainesville, FL 32607

International Iguana Society
Rt. 3, Box 328
Big Pine Key, FL 33043

Jacksonville Herpetological
  Society
P.O. Box 26468
Jacksonville, FL 32226-6468

Manasota Herpetological Society
P.O. Box 20381
Bradenton, FL 34203-0381

Palm Beach County
  Herpetological Society
P.O. Box 125
Loxahatchee, FL 33470

Save A Turtle
P.O. Box 361
Islamorada, FL 33036

Sawgrass Herpetological Society
P.O. Box 4852
Margate, FL 33063

Sea Turtle Preservation Society
P.O. Box 510988
Melbourne Beach, FL 32951

South Marion Herpetological
  Society
P.O. Box 1817
Bellview, FL 32620

Suncoast Herpetological Society
P.O. Box 2725
Dunedin, FL 34698
(813) 736-1368

Treasure Coast Herpetological
  Society
P.O. Box 65054
Vero Beach, FL 32965

Turtle and Tortoise Club of
  Florida
P.O. Box 239
Sanford, FL 32772-0239

United Herpetoculturists
  Network
P.O. Box 8400
Pompano Beach, FL 33075

West Florida Herpetological
  Society
3055 Panama Rd.
Pensacola, FL 32526

Georgia

Georgia Herpetological Society
Department of Herpetology, Zoo
  Atlanta
800 Cherokee Ave., SE
Atlanta, GA 30315

Marine Turtle Newsletter
Mercer University Biology
1400 Coleman Ave.
Macon, GA 31207

Troup County Herpetological
  Association
801 Grant St.
La Grange, GA 30240

Idaho

Idaho Herpetological Society
P.O. Box 6329
Boise, ID 83707

Illinois

Central Illinois Herpetological
  Society
1125 W. Lake Ave.
Peoria, IL 61614

Chicago Herpetological Society
2001 N. Clark St.
Chicago, IL 60614
(312) 281-1800,
   Fax (312) 549-5199

Reptiles R Us
P.O. Box 691
Glenview, IL 60025-0691

Indiana

Hossler Herpetological Society
P.O. Box 40544
Indianapolis, IN 46204

Mid-Mississippi Valley
   Herpetological Society
925 Park Place Dr.
Evansville, IN 47715

Iowa

Iowa Herpetological Society
P.O. Box 166
Norwalk, IA 50211

Kansas

Kansas Herpetological Society
Museum of Natural History
University of Kansas
Lawrence, KS 66045

Kaw Valley Herpetological
   Society
Rt. 1, Box 29B
Eudora, KS 66025

National Crotalus Society
P.O. Box 4
Onaga, KS 66521

Society for the Study of
   Amphibians and Reptiles
P.O. Box 626
Hays, KS 67601-0626
(913) 628-1437

Kentucky

Central Kentucky Herpetological
   Society
P.O. Box 12227
Lexington, KY 40581-2227

Kentucky Herpetological Society
102 Fourth St.
Nicholasville, KY 40358

Louisiana

Louisiana Herpetological Society
Museum of Natural History
Foster Hall, L.S.U.
Baton Rouge, LA 70803

Maryland

Maryland Herpetological Society
Natural History Society
2643 N. Charles St.
Baltimore, MD 21218

Western Maryland
   Herpetological Society
301 S. Main St.
Boonesboro, MD 21713

Massachusetts

New England Herpetological
   Society
P.O. Box 1082
Boston, MA 02103
(617) 789-5800

Michigan

Great Lakes Herpetological
   Society
13862 Church Rd.
Berville, MI 48002

Herpetological Society of
   Southwest Michigan
2557 Bristol, NW
Grand Rapids, MI 49504

Herptiles Out to Society
P.O. Box 12252
Hamtramck, MI 48212

Michigan Herpetological Society
Alma Tropical Fish
228 E. Superior St.
Alma, MI 48801

Michigan Society of
   Herpetologists
321 W. Oakland
Lansing, MI 48906
(517) 372-5730

Minnesota

Minnesota Herpetological
   Society
Bell Museum of Natural History
10 Church St., S.E.
Minneapolis, MN 55455-0104

Mississippi

Southern Mississippi
   Herpetological Society
P.O. Box 1685
Ocean Springs, MS 39564

Missouri

St. Louis Herpetological Society
P.O. Box 220153
Kirkwood, MO 63122

Nevada

Northern Nevada Herpetological
   Society
P.O. Box 21282
Reno, NV 89502-1282

Tortoise Group
5157 Poncho Circle
Las Vegas, NV 89119

New Jersey

Association for the Conservation
   of Turtles and Tortoises
RD 4, Box 368
Sussex, NJ 07461

Turtle Back Zoo
560 Northfield Ave.
West Orange, NJ 07052

New Mexico

Chihuahuan Desert
   Herpetological Society
Box 3 AF
New Mexico State University
Las Cruces, NM 88003

New Mexico Herpetological
   Society
University of New Mexico
Dept. of Biology
Albuquerque, NM 87131

New York

Long Island Herpetological
   Society
476 N. Ontario Ave.
Lindenhurst, NY 11757

New York Herpetological Society
P.O. Box 1245, Grand Central
   Station
New York, NY 10163-1245

New York Turtle and Tortoise
   Society
P.O. Box 878RA
Orange, NJ 07051-0878
(212) 459-4803

Upstate Herpetological
   Association
HCR 68, Box 30-B
Springfield Center, NY 13468
(518) 966-8192

North Carolina

Carolina Exotic Wildlife Society
Rt. 1, Box 396-C
Bethel, NC 27812

North Carolina Herpetological
  Society
State Museum
P.O. Box 29555
Raleigh, NC 27626
(919) 733-7450

Ohio

Central Ohio Herpetological
  Society
217 E. New England Ave.
Worthington, OH 43085

Greater Dayton Herpetological
  Society
Dayton Museum of Natural
  History
2629 Ridge Ave.
Dayton, OH 45414

Greater Cincinnati
  Herpetological Society
Cincinnati Museum of Natural
  History
1720 Gilbert Ave.
Cincinnati, OH 45202

Mid-Ohio Herpetological Society
P.O. Box 218331
Columbus, OH 43221

Northern Ohio Association of
  Herpetologists
Dept. of Biology
Cleveland Western Reserve
  University
Cleveland, OH 44106

Toledo Herpetological Society
1587 Jermain Dr.
Toledo, OH 43606
(419) 475-0521

Oklahoma

Oklahoma Herpetological
  Society

  Tulsa Chapter
  5701 E. 36 St. N
  Tulsa, OK 74115

  Oklahoma City Chapter
  Oklahoma Zoo, 2101 NE 50th
  Oklahoma City, OK 73111

Oregon

Oregon Herpetological Society
WISTEC P.O. Box 1518
Eugene, OR 97440

Pennsylvania

Lehigh Valley Herpetological
  Society
P.O. Box 9171
Allentown, PA 18105-9171

Philadelphia Herpetological
  Society
P.O. Box 52261
Philadelphia, PA 19115

Susquehanna Herp Society
211 S. Market St.
Muncy, PA 17756

Pittsburgh Herp Society
Pittsburgh Zoo, 1 Hill Rd.
Pittsburgh, PA 15206
(412) 361-0835

Rhode Island

Rhode Island Herpetological
  Association
30 Metropolitan Rd.
Providence, RI 02909
(401) 751-2807

South Carolina

Coastal Carolina Herpetocultural
  Society
#12, 6825 Dorchester Rd.
Charleston, SC 29418
(803) 767-2875

South Carolina Herpetological
  Society
P.O. Box 100107
Columbia, SC 29230

Turtle and Tortoise Society of
  Charleston
121 Hamlet Rd.
Summerville, SC 29485

Texas

East Texas Herpetological
  Society
RR2, Box 25 H
Trinity, TX 75862-9470

East Texas Regional
  Herpetological Society
314 Lynch Dr.
Bullard, TX 75757

El Paso Herpetological Society
7505 Dempsy
El Paso, TX 79925

Greater San Antonio
  Herpetological Society
134 Aldrich St.
San Antonio, TX 78227

HEART
Box 681231
Houston, TX 77268-1231

Herpetologists' League
Texas Parks and Wildlife
4200 Smith School Rd.
Austin, TX 78744

Horned Lizard Conservation
  Society
P.O. Box 122
Austin, TX 78767

Lubbock Turtle and Tortoise
  Society
5708 64 St.
Lubbock, TX 79424

North Texas Herpetological
  Society
P.O. Box 1043
Euless, TX 76039

South/Central Texas
  Herpetological Society
1405 Rabb Rd.
Austin, TX 78704

Texas Herpetological Society
Hutchinson Hall of Science
31 at Cantan
Lubbock, TX 79410

Utah

Utah Association of
  Herpetologists
195 W. 200 N.
Logan, UT 84321-3905

Utah Herpetological Society
Hogle Zoo
P.O. Box 8475
Salt Lake City, UT 84108

Virginia

Blue Ridge Herpetological
  Society
P.O. Box 727
Brookneal, VA 24528

Washington D.C. Herpetological
  Society
12420 Rock Ridge Rd.
Herndon, VA 22070

Washington

Pacific Northwest Herpetological
  Society
P.O. Box 70231
Bellevue, WA 98008

Wisconsin

Wisconsin Herpetological
  Society
P.O. Box 366
Germantown, WI 53022

Wyoming

Wahsatch Alliance of
  Herpetoculturists
T.A.H.P.O. Box 1907
Casper, WY 82602

Africa

Herpetological Association of
  Africa
Natural Museum
P.O. Box 266
9300 Bloemfontein
Republic of South Africa

Australia

Cape York Herpetological
  Society
Cook Highway
Palm Cove, Queensland 4879
Australia

Reptile Keepers Association
Box 98
Gosford, New South Wales 2250
Australia

Victorian Herpetological Society
16 Suspension St.
Ardeer, Victoria 3022
Australia

Austria

Österreichisches
  Herpetologisches Sammlung
Naturhistorisches Museum
Wien, Burgring 7
Postfach 417A 1014 Wien
Austria

Brazil

Instituto Butantan
Biblioteca A.V.
Vital Brasil
1400 Caixa
Postal 65 05504 São Paulo SP
Brazil

Canada

Association of Reptile Keepers
Sapperton RPO, P.O. Box 43020
New Westminster, BC
Canada V3L 5P7

Amphibian News Quarterly
RR 1
Limehouse, Ontario
Canada L0P 1H0

Canadian Terrapin Association
37 Shaw Crescent Barrie
Ontario
Canada L4N 4Z3
(705) 726-7363

Ontario Herpetological Society
P.O. Box 244
Port Credit, Ontario
Canada L5G 4L8

FOREIGN SOCIETIES

T.A.R.H.S.
Box 33083
3919 Richmond Rd.
SW Calgary, Alberta
Canada T3E 7E2

France

Société Herpétologique de France
Université de Paris VII
Laboratoire d'Anatomie
    Comparée
2 Place Jussieu, 75230 Paris
France

Germany

Deutsche Gesellschaft für
    Herpetologie und
    Terrarienkunde
Natur-Museum und
    Forschungsinstitut
    Senckenberg
Senckenberg-Anlage 25
Frankfurt-am-Main 6000
Germany

Naturhistoriches Museum
PSF 44, Bertholdsburg
Schleusingen 6056
Germany

India

Madras Crocodile Bank Trust
Post Bag Number 4
Mahabalipuram 603 104 Tamil
    Nadu
India

Netherlands

European Snake Society
Pauwenveld 18
De Zoetermeer 2727
Netherlands

Italy

Italian Herpetological Society
Via Lencavallo 57/C
Torino 1054
Italy

New Zealand

N.Z. Herpetological Society
50 Pupuke Rd.
Birkenhead, Auckland
New Zealand

N.Z. Herpetological Association
4 Craddock St.
Avondale, Auckland 7
New Zealand

Russia

Institute of Scientific
    Information
Academy of Sciences of USSR
Baltijskaya ul
Moscow 14 A-219
Russia

Russian Herpetological Society
Folium Publishing Company
58 Dmitrovskoe shossé
Moscow 127238
Russia
7-095-482-5590

Moscow Zoopark
Reptile Curator
123820 Moscow B
Gruzinskaya 1
Russia

Spain

Museo Nacional de Ciencias
José Gutiérrez Abascal
2 28006 Madrid
Spain

United Kingdom

Amphibian, Reptile and Insect
    Association
23 Windmill Rd.
Irthlingsborough Wellingborough
England NN9 5RJ

Association for the Study of
    Reptilia and Amphibia
Cotswold Wildlife Park
Burford Oxfordshire
England OX8 4JW

British Association of Tortoise
    Keepers
Edgbaston Hotel
323 Hagley Rd.
Birmingham
England B178 ND

British Dendrobatid Group
5 Richards Rd.
Standish Wigan
England WN6 0QU

British Herpetological Society
Zoological Society of London
Regents Park London
England NW1 4RY

East Sussex Herpetological
    Society
20 Silverlands Rd.
St. Lenards-on-Sea
East Sussex
England
(0424) 440895

Reptiles and Amphibians Society
S. Churchman
85 Devon Rd.
Barking, Essex
England
(081) 5913067

International Herpetological
    Society
65 Broadstone Ave.
Walsall West Midlands
England WS3 1JA

Eastern Herpetological Society
113 Thunder Lane
Norwich, Norfolk
England NR7 0JG

Milton Keynes Herpetological
    Society
B. Pomfret
15 Esk Way
Bletchley Milton Keynes
England MK3 7PW

National Association of Private
    Animal Keepers
1 Manor Cottage
Station Rd.
Stoke d'Abermon Cobham
England KT11 3BW
(0932) 866243

Portsmouth Reptile and
    Amphibian Society
39 Wykeham Rd.
Wickham Hants
England PO17 5AD

International Herpetological
    Society

    Kent Branch
    Herne Bay Angling Association
        H.Q.
    59 Central Parade
    Herne Bay
    England

    East Anglian Branch
    8 Branford Lane
    Ipswich
    Suffolk
    England IP1 4DA

Shropshire Herpetological
    Society
55 Boscobel
Dr. Heath Farm
Shrewsbury Shropshire
England

Scottish Herpetological Society
2 New Houses
Garvald East Lothian
Scotland EH41 4LN

Three Counties Reptilians
34 King John's Rd.
N Warnborough Basingstoke
England RG23 1EJ
(0256) 702543

Wirral Herpetological Society
4 Elm Park Rd.
Wallasey, Wirral
England L45 5JH

Venezuela

Asociación Venezolana de
  Herpetología
Apartado de Correo 567
Valencia 2001/A
Venezuela

COLLEGES AND UNIVERSITIES

Arizona

Arizona State University
Dept. of Biological Sciences
Life Sciences Bldg.
Tempe, AZ 85287

University of Arizona
Ecology and Evolutionary
  Biology
1313 E. South Campus Dr.
Tucson, AZ 85721
(602) 621-7630, 621-3107

California

University of California at Davis
Section of Evolution and Ecology
Davis, CA 95616

Colorado

Colorado State University
Dept. of Biology
Fort Collins, CO 80523
(303) 491-5376

University of Colorado at
  Boulder
Dept. of Biology
Campus Box 30
Boulder, CO 80309-0030

Florida

University of Miami
Dept. of Biology
P.O. Box 248025
Coral Gables, FL 33124

Georgia

University of Georgia
Museum of Natural Resources,
  Dept. of Ecology
Athens, GA 30602

Illinois

Southern Illinois University
Dept. of Zoology
Carbondale, IL 62901-6501

Kansas

University of Kansas
Museum of Natural History
Lawrence, KS 66045-2454

Kentucky

Eastern Kentucky University
Dept. of Biology
Richmond, KY 40475-3124

Louisiana

Louisiana State University
Museum of Natural Science
Baton Rouge, LA 70803

Massachusetts

Harvard University
Graduate School of Arts and
  Sciences
Dept. of Biology
Cambridge, MA 02138

University of Massachusetts
Organismic and Evolutionary
  Biology
Morrill Science Center
Amherst, MA 01003-0027

Michigan

Michigan State University
Zoology Dept.
203 Natural Science Bldg.
E. Lansing, MI 48824

University of Michigan
Dept. of Biology
1220 Student Activities Bldg.
Ann Arbor, MI 48109

Missouri

University of Missouri at
  Columbia
218 Tucker Hall
Division of Biological Sciences
Columbia, MO 65211

Nebraska

University of Nebraska
Dept. of Biology
Omaha, NE 68182

New York

Cornell University
Dept. of Biology
410 Thurston Ave.
Ithaca, NY 14850

Pennsylvania

Pennsylvania State University
Dept. of Biology
201 Shields Bldg., Box 3000
University Park, PA 16802

Shippensburg University
Dept. of Biology
Shippensburg, PA 17257

Tennessee

University of Tennessee
Dept. of Zoology
Knoxville, TN 37996-0810

Texas

University of Texas at Arlington
Dept. of Biology
P.O. Box 19088
Arlington, TX 76019-0088

University of Texas at El Paso
Dept. of Biology
500 W. University Ave.
El Paso, TX 79968

Washington

University of Washington
Dept. of Zoology
Seattle, WA 98195

Washington State University
Dept. of Zoology
Pullman, WA 99164-4236

Wisconsin

University of Wisconsin
145 Noland Hall
250 N. Mills St.
Madison, WI 53706

Canada

University of Calgary
Dept. of Biology
Calgary, Alberta
Canada T2N 1N4

University of Guelph
Dept. of Zoology
Guelph, Ontario
Canada N1G 2W1

SELECTED REFERENCES

AN ASTERISK (*) marks references that provide information on endangered, threatened, and other protected species; these are grouped at the end of the listings for each region, state, etc. A dagger (†) marks references for which ordering information is available in the source directory immediately following this bibliography.

GENERAL

Bartlett, Richard D. *In Search of Reptiles and Amphibians.* New York: E. J. Brill, 1988.

Behler, John L., and F. Wayne King. *The Audubon Society Field Guide to North American Reptiles and Amphibians.* New York: Alfred A. Knopf, 1979.

Collins, Joseph T. *Standard Common and Current Scientific Names for North American Reptiles and Amphibians.* 3d ed. N.p.: Society for the Study of Amphibians and Reptiles, 1990.

Ditmars, Raymond L. *The Reptiles of North America.* New York: Doubleday & Company, Inc., 1951.

Ernst, Carl H. *Venomous Reptiles of North America.* Washington, D.C.: Smithsonian Institution Press, 1992.

Kauffeld, Carl F. *Snakes and Snake Hunting.* Garden City, N.Y.: Hanover House, 1957.

Klauber, Laurence M. *Rattlesnakes: Their Habits, Life Histories, and Influence on Mankind.* Abridged ed. Berkeley and Los Angeles: Univ. of California Press, 1982.

Markel, Ronald G. *Kingsnakes and Milk Snakes.* Neptune City, N.J.: T.F.H. Publications, Inc., 1990.

Means, Bruce. *Diamonds in the Rough.* Tallahassee, Fla.: Coastal Plains Institute, n.d.

Seigel, Richard A., Joseph T. Collins, and Susan S. Novak. *Snakes: Ecology and Evolutionary Biology.* New York: Macmillan, 1987.

Smith, H. M., and E. D. Brodie, Jr. *Reptiles of North America.* New York: Golden Press, 1982.

Tyning, Thomas F. *A Guide to Amphibians and Reptiles.* Boston: Little, Brown, & Company, 1990.

Wright, Albert Hazen, and Anna Allen Wright. *Handbook of Snakes of the United States and Canada.* 3 vols. including bibliography. Ithaca, N.Y.: Comstock Publishing Associates, 1957.

*U.S. Dept. of the Interior, Fish and Wildlife Service. Endangered and Threatened Wildlife and Plants; Animal Candidate Review for Listing as Endangered or Threatened Species, Proposed Rule. *Federal Register*, Part VIII, 1991.

*———. Endangered and Threatened Wildlife and Plants. 50 CFR 17.11 and 17.12, 1992.

REGIONAL

New England

DeGraaf, Richard M., and Deborah D. Rudis. *Amphibians and Reptiles of New England.* Amherst: Univ. of Massachusetts Press, 1983.

Eastern/Central

Conant, Roger, and Joseph T. Collins. *Reptiles and Amphibians of Eastern and Central North America.* Peterson Field Guide series. Boston: Houghton Mifflin Company, 1991.

Jackson, Jeffrey J. *Snakes of the Southeastern United States.* Athens: Univ. of Georgia, 1983.

Martof, Bernard S., William M. Palmer, Joseph R. Bailey, and Julian R. Harrison III. *Amphibians and Reptiles of the Carolinas and Virginia.* Chapel Hill: Univ. of North Carolina Press, 1980.

Western

Shaw, C. E., and S. Campbell. *Snakes of the American West.* New York: Alfred A. Knopf, 1974.

Stebbins, Robert C. *Western Reptiles and Amphibians.* Peterson Field Guide series. Boston: Houghton Mifflin Company, 1985.

Pacific Northwest

Nussbaum, Ronald A., Edmund D. Brodie, Jr., and Robert M. Storm. *Amphibians and Reptiles of the Pacific Northwest.* Moscow: Univ. of Idaho Press, 1983.

Canada

Cook, Francis R. *Introduction to Canadian Amphibians and Reptiles.* Ottawa: Natl. Mus. of Canada, 1984.

Froom, Barbara. *The Snakes of Canada.* Toronto: McClelland and Stewart, Ltd., 1972.

STATES

Alabama

Linzey, Donald W. *Snakes of Alabama.* Huntsville: Strode Publishers, 1979.

Arizona

Hardy, David L., Sr., M.D., ed. *Collected Papers of the Tucson
  Herpetological Society.* Tucson: Tucson Herpetological Society,
  1992.
Lowe, Charles H., Cecil R. Schwalbe, and Terry B. Johnson. *The
  Venomous Reptiles of Arizona.* Phoenix: Arizona Game and
  Fish Dept., 1986.
*Arizona Game and Fish Commission. Threatened Native Wild-
  life in Arizona. Phoenix, 1988.
* †U.S. Fish and Wildlife Service, Ecological Services Field Office.
  Endangered and Threatened Species of Arizona. Phoenix, 1991.

Arkansas

Dowling, Herndon G. *A Review of the Amphibians and Reptiles
  of Arkansas.* Occasional Papers No. 3. Fayetteville: Univ. of
  Arkansas Mus., 1957.
*Arkansas Game and Fish Commission. Arkansas's List of Endan-
  gered and Threatened Species. Little Rock, 1992.

California

* †California Dept. of Fish and Game. California Threatened and
  Endangered Species List. Sacramento, 1992.

Colorado

Hammerson, Geoffrey A. *Amphibians and Reptiles in Colorado.*
  Denver: Colorado Division of Wildlife, Dept. of Natural Resources, 1982.

Colorado

*Colorado Dept. of Natural Resources, Division of Wildlife. Wild-
  life in Danger: The Status of Colorado's Threatened or Endangered Fish, Amphibians, Birds, and Mammals. Denver, 1989.

Connecticut

Petersen, Richard C., and Robert W. Fritsch, II. *Connecticut's
  Venomous Snakes.* State Geolog. and Natur. Hist. Survey Bull.
  No. 111. Hartford: 1986.
* †State of Connecticut, Dept. of Environmental Protection,
  Natural Resources Center, Natural Diversity Data Base. Con-
  necticut's Endangered, Threatened, and Species Concern Spe-
  cies. Hartford, 1992.

Delaware

*State of Delaware, Dept. of Natural Resources and Environmental Control, Division of Fish and Wildlife. Delaware Official List of Threatened and Endangered Wildlife Species. Dover, n.d. (no snakes listed)

Florida

Ashton, Ray E., Jr., and Patricia Sawyer Ashton. *Handbook of Reptiles and Amphibians of Florida.* Part 1, *The Snakes.* 2d ed. Miami: Windward Publishing, 1988.

Duellman, William E., and Albert Schwartz. *Amphibians and Reptiles of Southern Florida.* Bull. of the Florida State Mus. No. 3. Gainesville: 1958.

*Florida Game and Fresh Water Fish Commission. Don Wood, comp. Official Lists of Endangered and Potentially Endangered Fauna and Flora in Florida. Tallahassee, 1992.

McDiarmid, Roy W. *Rare and Endangered Biota of Florida,* vol. 111, *Amphibians and Reptiles.* Gainesville: Univ. Presses of Florida, 1978.

Wilson, Larry David, and Louis Parras. *The Ecological Impact of Man on the South Florida Herpetofauna.* Univ. of Kansas Mus. Natur. Hist. Special Pub. No. 9. Lawrence, 1983.

Georgia

Martof, Bernard S. *Amphibians and Reptiles of Georgia.* Athens: Univ. of Georgia Press, 1956.

* †Georgia Dept. of Natural Resources, Nongame Wildlife Program. Georgia's Protected Species. Forsyth, 1992.

Idaho

* †Idaho Dept. of Fish and Game, Nongame and Endangered Wildlife Program, Conservation Data Center. Rare, Threatened, and Endangered Plants and Animals of Idaho. Boise, 1992.

Illinois

Smith, Philip W. The Amphibians and Reptiles of Illinois. *Illinois Natural History Survey* 28, Art.1. Urbana, 1979.

* †Illinois Endangered Species Protection Board. Checklist of Endangered and Threatened Animals and Plants of Illinois. Springfield, 1990.

Indiana

Minton, Sherman A., Jr. *Amphibians and Reptiles of Indiana.* Monograph No. 3. Indianapolis: Indiana Academy of Science, 1972.

* †Indiana Division of Fish and Wildlife. Eye on Wildlife, Rare
  Species Report. Indianapolis, n.d.

Iowa

Christiansen, James L., and Reeve M. Bailey. *The Snakes of Iowa.*
  Des Moines: Iowa Conservation Commission, 1986.
*Christiansen, James L., and Russell R. Burken. *The Endangered
  and Uncommon Reptiles and Amphibians of Iowa.* Cedar Falls:
  Iowa Academy of Science, 1978.

Kansas

Collins, Joseph T. *Amphibians and Reptiles in Kansas.* 2d ed.
  Univ. of Kansas Mus. Natur. Hist. Public Edu. Ser. No. 8. Lawrence, 1982.
* †Kansas Dept. of Wildlife and Parks. Kansas Threatened and Endangered Species. Emporia, 1992.

Kentucky

Barbour, Roger W. *Amphibians and Reptiles of Kentucky.* Lexing-
  ton: Univ. Press of Kentucky, 1971.
*Babcock, Jan V. *Endangered Plants and Animals of Kentucky.*
  Lexington: College of Engineering, Univ. of Kentucky, 1977.
* †Kentucky Dept. of Fish and Wildlife Resources. Threatened and
  Endangered Species. *Kentucky Afield Magazine* (March/April
  1993) 24.
*Kentucky State Nature Preserves Commission. Endangered,
  Threatened, and Special Concern Plant and Animal Species of
  Kentucky. Frankfort, 1991.

Louisiana

Dundee, Harold A., and Douglas A. Rossman. *The Reptiles and
  Amphibians of Louisiana.* Baton Rouge: Louisiana State Univ.
  Press, 1989.
*Louisiana Dept. of Wildlife and Fisheries. Animals Listed as
  Threatened/Endangered in Louisiana. Baton Rouge, 1991.
*Louisiana Natural Heritage Program. Special Animals. Baton
  Rouge, 1990.

Maine

*Maine Dept. of Inland Fisheries and Wildlife. The Maine Endan-
  gered and Nongame Wildlife Fund (newsletter). Winter 92–93.
*Maine Dept. of Inland Fisheries and Wildlife. Wildlife Division,
  Research and·Management Report. Augusta, 1992.

Maryland

Harris, Herbert S., Jr. Distributional Survey (Amphibia/Reptilia): Maryland and the District of Columbia. *Bull. Maryland Herpetol. Soc.* 11, no. 3. (1975).

* †Maryland Natural Heritage Program, Resource Conservation Service, Dept. of Natural Resources. Rare, Threatened, and Endangered Animals of Maryland. Annapolis, 1992.

Massachusetts

* †Commonwealth of Massachusetts, Division of Fisheries and Wildlife. Massachusetts List of Endangered, Threatened, and Special Concern Species. Boston, 1992.

Michigan

Holman, J. Alan, James H. Harding, Marvin M. Hensley, and Glenn R. Dudderar. *Michigan Snakes: A Field Guide and Pocket Reference.* East Lansing: Michigan State Univ. Mus. and Coop. Ext. Serv., 1989.

*Michigan Dept. of Natur. Res., Wildlife and Fisheries Division. Endangered and Threatened Species. Lansing, 1991.

Minnesota

Lang, Jeffrey W. *The Reptiles and Amphibians of Minnesota: Distribution Maps, Habitat Preferences, and Selected References.* Minnesota Dept. of Natural Resources, 1982.

*Minnesota Dept. of Natural Resources, Nongame Wildlife and Natural Heritage Programs. The Uncommon Ones: Minnesota's Endangered Plants and Animals. MDNR, 1989.

Mississippi

Lohoefener, Renne R., and Ronald Altig. *Mississippi Herpetology.* Mississippi State Univ. Research Ctr. Bull. No. 1. NSTL Station, 1983.

* †Mississippi Dept. of Wildlife, Fisheries and Parks, Museum of Natural Resources, Mississippi Natural Heritage Program. Special Animals. Jackson, 1993.

Missouri

Johnson, Tom R. *The Amphibians and Reptiles of Missouri.* Jefferson City: Missouri Dept. of Conservation, 1987.

*Missouri Dept. of Conservation. Rare and Endangered Species of Missouri. Jefferson City, 1984, 1992.

Montana

Thompson, Larry S. *Distribution of Montana Amphibians, Rep-
tiles, and Mammals.* Helena: Montana Game and Fish, 1982.
* †Montana Dept. of Fish, Wildlife, and Parks. Endangered Species
List. Helena, 1991 (no snakes included).

Nebraska

Lynch, John D. Annotated Checklist of the Amphibians and Rep-
tiles of Nebraska. *Trans. Nebraska Acad. Sci.* 13 (1985).
* Nebraska Game and Parks Commission. Preserving a Priceless
Heritage: Nebraska's Nongame and Endangered Species Pro-
gram. Lincoln, 1990.
* †Nebraska Game and Parks Commission, Wildlife Division.
Nebraska's Vanishing Species. Lincoln, 1992.

Nevada

* Nevada Dept. of Wildlife. Protected Fish and Wildlife Species of
Nevada. Reno, n.d.

New Hampshire

Oliver, James A., and Joseph R. Bailey. *Amphibians and Reptiles
of New Hampshire.* Concord: Biol. Survey of the Connecticut
Watershed, 1939.
* †New Hampshire Fish and Game Dept., Nongame and Endan-
gered Wildlife Program. Species Occurring in New Hampshire.
Concord, 1992.

New Jersey

Trapido, Harold. *The Snakes of New Jersey: A Guide.* Newark:
Newark Mus., 1937.
* †New Jersey Dept. of Environmental Protection and Energy, Di-
vision of Fish, Game, and Wildlife, Endangered and Nongame
Species Program. Endangered and Threatened Wildlife of New
Jersey. Hampton, N.J., 1992.

New Mexico

* Baltosser, William H., Howard Campbell, J. William Eley, John P.
Hubbard, and C. Gregory Schmitt. *Handbook of Species Endan-
gered in New Mexico.* Santa Fe: New Mexico Dept. of Game and
Fish, 1985.
* †New Mexico Dept. of Game and Fish. Amended Listing of En-
dangered Wildlife of New Mexico. Santa Fe, 1990.

New York

* †New York State Dept. of Environmental Conservation, Division of Fish and Wildlife, Wildlife Resources Center. Endangered, Threatened, and Special Concern Fish and Wildlife of New York State. Delmar, N.Y., 1993.

North Carolina

Palmer, William M. *Poisonous Snakes of North Carolina.* Raleigh: State Mus. of Natural History, 1974.
* North Carolina Wildlife Resources Commission. Endangered Wildlife of North Carolina. Raleigh, 1992.

North Dakota

Wheeler, George C., and Jeanette Wheeler. *The Amphibians and Reptiles of North Dakota.* Grand Forks: Univ. of North Dakota Press, 1966.
* †North Dakota State Game and Fish Dept. The Rare Ones. *North Dakota Outdoors Magazine* 49, no. 2 (August 1986).

Ohio

Conant, Roger. *The Reptiles of Ohio.* 2d ed. Notre Dame, Ind.: University of Notre Dame Press, 1951.
* Ohio Dept. of Natural Resources, Division of Wildlife. Ohio's Endangered Wild Animals. Columbus, 1991.

Oklahoma

Sievert, Gregory, and Lynnette Sievert. *A Field Guide to the Reptiles of Oklahoma.* Oklahoma City: Oklahoma Dept. of Wildlife Conservation, 1988.
* †Oklahoma Dept. of Wildlife Conservation. Oklahoma's Endangered Species. Oklahoma City: ODWC, 1992.

Oregon

St. John, A. D. *Knowing Oregon Reptiles.* Salem: Salem Audubon Society, 1980.
* †Oregon Dept. of Fish and Wildlife. Oregon List of Threatened and Endangered Species, and List of Sensitive Species. Portland, 1993.

Pennsylvania

McCoy, C. J. *Amphibians and Reptiles in Pennsylvania: Checklist, Bibliography, and Atlas of Distribution.* Carnegie Mus. Natur. Hist. Special Pub. No. 6. Pittsburgh, 1982.

*Pennsylvania Fish and Boat Commission, Division of Fisheries
    Management. Pennsylvania Fishing and Boating Regulations.
    Bellefonte, 1993. Endangered Species, p. 93.

Rhode Island

*Rhode Island Dept. of Environmental Management, Division of
    Fish and Wildlife. Rhode Island Natural Heritage Program. *In
    Danger of Being Lost Forever.* West Kingston, n.d.

South Carolina

*Listed Reptile and Amphibian Species of South Carolina.

South Dakota

Melius, Michael M. *Plants and Animals Rare in South Dakota: A
    Field Guide.* Hermosa: Ornate Press, 1987.
Over, William H. *Amphibians and Reptiles of South Dakota.*
    South Dakota Geol. and Natur. Hist. Survey Bull. No. 12. Ver-
    million: 1923.

Tennessee

Sinclair, Ralph, Will Hon, and Robert B. Ferguson. *Amphibians
    and Reptiles in Tennessee.* Nashville: Tennessee Game and Fish
    Commission, 1965.
* †Tennessee Wildlife Resources Agency. Endangered and Threat-
    ened Wildlife Species of Tennessee. Jackson, n.d.

Texas

Dixon, James R. *Amphibians and Reptiles of Texas.* College Sta-
    tion: Texas A&M Univ. Press, 1987.
Garrett, Judith M., and David G. Barker. *A Field Guide to Reptiles
    and Amphibians of Texas.* Austin: Texas Monthly Press, 1987.
Tennant, Alan. *The Snakes of Texas.* Austin: Texas Monthly
    Press, 1984.
Vermersch, Thomas G., and Robert E. Kuntz. *Snakes of South
    Central Texas.* Austin: Eakin Press, 1986.
* †Texas Parks and Wildlife Dept. *Texas Hunting Guide, 1992–
    1993.* Austin: Blackford Co., 1992.

Utah

* †Dept. of Natural Resources, Utah Division of Wildlife Re-
    sources. Native Utah Wildlife Species of Special Concern. Salt
    Lake City, 1987.

Vermont

*Vermont Dept. of Fish and Wildlife, Nongame and Heritage Program. Endangered and Threatened Animals of Vermont. VDFW, 1992.

Virginia

Linzey, Donald W., and Michael J. Clifford. *Snakes of Virginia.* Charlottesville: Univ. Press of Virginia, 1981.

Tobey, Franklin J. *Virginia's Amphibians and Reptiles: A Distributional Survey.* Purcellville: Virginia Herpetological Society, 1985.

*Virginia Dept. of Game and Inland Fisheries. Endangered and Threatened Species in Virginia. VDGIF, 1993.

Washington

* †Washington Dept. of Wildlife. Endangered and Threatened: 1991. Status Report. Olympia, 1991.

West Virginia

Green, N. Bayard, and Thomas K. Pauley. *Amphibians and Reptiles in West Virginia.* Pittsburgh: Univ. of Pittsburgh Press, 1987.

* †Division of Natural Resources, Nongame Wildlife Program. Threatened and Endangered Wildlife in West Virginia. Elkins, 1991.

Wisconsin

Vogt, Richard Carl. *Natural History of Amphibians and Reptiles of Wisconsin.* Milwaukee: Milwaukee Public Mus., 1981.

* †Wisconsin Dept. of Natural Resources, Wisconsin Natural Heritage Program, Bureau of Endangered Resources. Wisconsin Natural Heritage Working Lists. Madison, 1993.

Wyoming

Baxter, George T., and Michael D. Stone. *Amphibians and Reptiles of Wyoming.* 2d ed. Cheyenne: Wyoming Fish and Game Dept., 1985.

* †Wyoming Game and Fish Dept. Wyoming's Endangered Species. Cheyenne, n.d.

SOURCE DIRECTORY

California Department of Fish
and Game
P.O. Box 944209
Sacramento CA 94244-2090

Coastal Plains Institute
1313 N. Duval Street
Tallahassee FL 32303

Colorado Dept. of Natural
Resources
Division of Wildlife
6060 Broadway
Denver CO 80216

State of Connecticut
Dept. of Environmental
Protection
Natural Resources Center
165 Capitol Avenue, Room #553
Hartford CT 06106

State of Delaware
Department of Natural
Resources and Environmental
Control
Division of Fish and Wildlife
89 King's Highway
P.O. Box 1401
Dover DE 19903

Georgia Department of Natural
Resources
Nongame Wildlife Program
Route 3, Box 180
Forsyth GA 31029

Idaho Department of Fish and
Game
Nongame and Endangered
Wildlife Program
Conservation Data Center
P.O. Box 25
Boise ID 83707

Illinois Endangered Species
Protection Board
Lincoln Tower Plaza
524 South Second
Springfield IL 62701-1787

Indiana Division of Fish and
Wildlife
402 West Washington St.
Room W273
Indianapolis IN 46204

Kansas Dept. of Wildlife and
Parks
P.O. Box 1525
Emporia KS 66801

Kentucky Dept. of Fish and
Wildlife Resources
#1 Game Farm Road
Frankfort KY 40601

Maryland Natural Heritage
Program
Resource Conservation Service
Dept. of Natural Resources
Tawes State Office Bldg.
Annapolis MD 21401

Commonwealth of
  Massachusetts
Division of Fisheries and Wildlife
100 Cambridge Street
Room 1902
Boston MA 02202

Mississippi Dept. of Wildlife
Fisheries and Parks
Museum of Natural Resources
111 N. Jefferson St.
Jackson MS 39202-2897

Montana Dept. of Fish, Wildlife,
  and Parks
1420 E. 6th Ave.
P.O. Box 200701
Helena MT 59620-0701

Nebraska Game and Parks
  Commission
Wildlife Division
P.O. Box 30370
Lincoln NE 68503

New Hampshire Fish and Game
  Dept.
Nongame and Endangered
  Wildlife Program
2 Hazon Drive
Concord NH 03301

New Jersey Dept. of
  Environmental Protection and
  Energy
Division of Fish, Game, and
  Wildlife
Endangered and Nongame
  Species Program
Northern District Office
Box 383 R.D. 1
Hampton NJ 08827

New Mexico Dept. of Game and
  Fish
State Capitol
408 Galisteo
Santa Fe NM 87503

New York State Dept. of
  Environmental Conservation
Division of Fish and Wildlife
Wildlife Resources Center
Delmar NY 12054

North Dakota State Game and
  Fish Dept.
100 N. Bismark Expressway
Bismark ND 58501-5095

Oklahoma Dept. of Wildlife
  Conservation
1801 N. Lincoln Blvd.
Oklahoma City OK 73105

Oregon Dept. of Fish and Wildlife
P.O. Box 59
2501 S.W. 1st Ave.
Portland OR 97207

Tennessee Wildlife Resources
  Agency
Region 1, Box 55
State Office Bldg.
225 Dr. Martin Luther King
  Drive
Jackson TN 38301

Texas Parks and Wildlife Dept.
4200 Smith School Road
Austin TX 78744

Dept. of Natural Resources
Utah Division of Wildlife
  Resources
1596 W. North Temple
Salt Lake City UT 84116-3195

Washington Dept. of Wildlife
600 Capitol Way
N. Olympia WA 98501-1091

Division of Natural Resources
Nongame Wildlife Program
P.O. Box 67
Elkins WV 26241

Wisconsin Dept. of Natural
  Resources
Wisconsin Natural Heritage
  Program
Bureau of Endangered Resources
Box 7921
Madison WI 53707

Wyoming Game and Fish Dept.
5400 Bishop Blvd.
Cheyenne WY 82006

INDEX

Boldface page numbers indicate principal references.